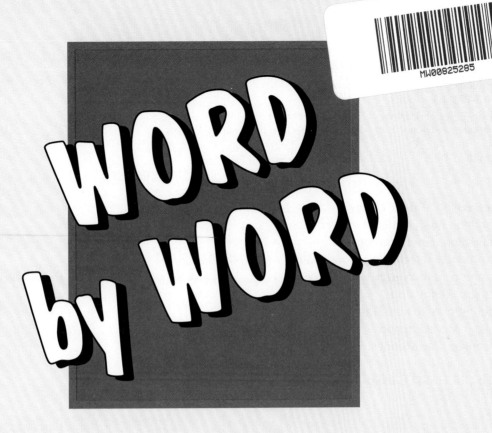

WORD by WORD

DICCIONARIO ILUSTRADO DE INGLÉS

English/Spanish Picture Dictionary

Steven J. Molinsky   Bill Bliss
Herlinda Charpentier Saitz

Longman

Library of Congress Cataloging-in-Publication Data

Molinsky, Steven J.
    Word by word picture dictionary. English/Spanish Picture Dictionary
  Steven J. Molinsky, Bill Bliss, Herlinda Charpentier Saitz
        p.   cm.
      Includes index.
      ISBN 0-13-125865-6 (pbk.)
        1. English language–Textbookls fpr foreign speakers—Spanish.
    2. English language—Dictionaries—Spanish. 3. Picture dictionaries, English.
    I. Bliss, Bill.   II. Title.
    PE1129.S8M48   1995   423'.61—dc20   95-718 CIP

Acquisitions editor: *Tina B. Carver*
Managing editor, production: *Dominick Mosco*
Production editor: *Janet Johnston*
Electronic production technology coordinator: *Molly Pike Riccardi*
Electronic production: *Steven K. Jorgensen*
Interior design: *Kenny Beck*
Cover supervisor: *Marianne Frasco*
Cover design: *Merle Krumper*
Buyer/scheduler: *Ray Keating*

Illustrated by RICHARD E. HILL

© 1995 by Prentice Hall Regents
A Pearson Education Company
Pearson Education
10 Bank Street
White Plains, NY 10606

Printed in the United States of America

20 19 18 17 16 15

ISBN 0-13-125865-6

ÍNDICE/CONTENIDO

El Diccionario ilustrado *Word by Word* contiene más de 3.000 palabras en ilustraciones de colores vívidos y ofrece el vocabulario esencial necesario para comunicarse efectivamente en una amplia variedad de situaciones y contextos.

Word by Word organiza cuidadosamente el vocabulario en 100 unidades temáticas con una secuencia de lecciones cuyos temas abarcan desde las experiencias más inmediatas al estudiante hasta aquellas pertinentes al mundo que lo rodea. A las primeras unidades, dedicadas a la familia, la casa, los hábitos y quehaceres domésticos siguen lecciones sobre la comunidad, la escuela, el trabajo, cómo ir de compras, formas de recreo y otras. *Word by Word* presenta en forma detallada desde materias y actividades escolares de rutina hasta importantes tópicos relacionados con la vida. *Word by Word* puede emplearse en la secuencia en que aparecen los temas o en cualquier otro orden que se desee.

Para mayor conveniencia en el manejo del manual los títulos de las unidades aparecen en el Contenido tal como aparecen en el texto y en el Índice temático se ordenan alfabéticamente. Las palabras, por su parte, se registran alfabéticamente en el Glosario con la intención de que tanto los estudiantes como los profesores puedan localizar fácil y rápidamente todas las palabras y los temas.

El diccionario ilustrado *Word by Word* es el texto central del *Programa completo de desarrollo de vocabulario* que comprende una extensa selección de materiales impresos y audiovisuales para la enseñanza del inglés en todos los niveles.

Los materiales auxiliares incluyen Cuadernos de ejercicios en tres niveles (alfabetización, primer nivel y nivel intermedio) dos manuales para el maestro (una guía didáctica y un manual con estrategias para la enseñanza del vocabulario), audiocintas, láminas, diapositivas a colores, un juego de vocabulario en tarjetas, un álbum de canciones con su propio libro y un programa de ejercicios de evaluación.

Estrategias didácticas

Word by Word presenta el vocabulario dentro de un contexto. Las palabras se usan en conversaciones modelo que reproducen con fidelidad su uso acostumbrado. Los modelos sirven de base para que los estudiantes se entreguen a prácticas de conversación interactivas y dinámicas. Además, en cada unidad hay preguntas de discusión y redacción para estimularlos a relacionar el vocabulario y los temas a sus propias vidas mientras comparten experiencias, pensamientos, opiniones e información sobre sí mismos, su cultura y sus países. De esta forma, los estudiantes llegan a conocerse "palabra por palabra".

Al usar *Word by Word* los animamos a desarrollar estrategias que sean compatibles con su propio estilo, y las necesidades y habilidades de sus estudiantes. Para presentar y practicar el vocabulario de cada unidad puede ser útil incorporar algunas de las siguientes técnicas.

1. *Preparación del vocabulario:* estimule el conocimiento previo del vocabulario que tengan los alumnos, ya sea provocándolos a que usen las palabras en la unidad que ellos ya conocen, escribiendo dichas palabras en la pizarra o haciendo que ellos miren las láminas, las diapositivas o las ilustraciones de Palabra por palabra e identifiquen aquellas con las que están familiarizados.

2. *Presentación del vocabulario:* señale la ilustración de cada palabra, repitiéndola en voz alta y haciendo que los alumnos la repitan en coro e individualmente. Tenga presente la necesidad de verificar la comprensión y pronunciación del vocabulario.

3. *Práctica del vocabulario:* haga que los alumnos practiquen el vocabulario en coro con usted, en parejas o en grupos pequeños. Pronuncie o escriba una palabra y haga que los estudiantes señalen la ilustración o digan el número que la acompaña. O, señale o diga el número correspondiente a una ilustración y haga que los alumnos pronuncien la palabra a que éste pertenece.

4. *Práctica de conversaciones modelo:* algunas unidades tienen conversaciones modelo que usan la primera palabra en la lista del vocabulario. Otras conversaciones modelo están en forma de diálogos esquemáticos en que se pueden insertar las palabras del vocabulario. En muchos diálogos esquemáticos hay números en corchetes que indican cuáles palabras pueden usarse para practicar la conversación. Si no aparecen números en corchetes, se pueden usar todas las palabras en la página.

Se recomiendan los siguientes pasos para la práctica de conversaciones modelo:

a. Presentación: los alumnos observan la ilustración e intercambian ideas sobre quiénes serán los que hablan y dónde tiene lugar la conversación

b. Se presenta y se verifica la comprensión de la situación y del vocabulario.

c. Los alumnos repiten cada línea de la conversación en coro o individualmente.

d. Los alumnos practican el modelo en parejas.

e. Una pareja de estudiantes presenta la conversación nueva basada en el modelo, usando diferentes palabras del vocabulario.

f. Basándose en el modelo, los alumnos, en parejas, practican varias conversaciones nuevas usando diferentes palabras del vocabulario.

g. Cada pareja presenta su diálogo al resto de la clase.

5. *Práctica de conversación adicional:* muchas unidades proveen dos diálogos esquemáticos adicionales para afianzar la práctica empleando el vocabulario de la unidad. (Éstas se encuentran sombreadas en amarillo al pie de la página). Haga que los alumnos practiquen y presenten estos diálogos usando cualquier palabra que deseen.

6. *Práctica de escritura y ortografía*: Haga que los alumnos practiquen deletreando las palabras en coro con usted, en pares o en grupos pequeños. Diga o deletree una palabra y luego haga que los alumnos la escriban y señalen la ilustración o el número que le corresponde. O, señale una ilustración o diga un número; luego haga que los alumnos escriban la palabra.

7. *Temas para discusión, composición, diarios y archivos:* todas las unidades en *Word by Word* suministran una o más preguntas que pueden servir para discutir o para escribir sobre el tema de la unidad. Éstas se encuentran en áreas sombreadas de verde al pie de la página. Haga que los alumnos respondan a las preguntas en clase, en pares o en grupos pequeños; o haga que los alumnos escriban sus respuestas en casa, compartan su composición con otros compañeros y las discutan en clase con los demás alumnos ya sea en pares o en grupos pequeños.

Los alumnos pueden interesarse en guardar un diario de su trabajo escrito. Si lo permite el tiempo, usted puede contestarle a cada uno, por escrito, compartiendo sus opiniones y experiencias o reaccionando a lo que ellos hayan escrito. Si usted archiva el trabajo escrito de sus alumnos, estas composiciones constituyen un excelente testimonio de su progreso y aprendizaje del inglés.

8. *Actividades comunicativas:* la guía didáctica provee innumerables maneras para estimular y provocar a los alumnos con la intención de aprovechar los diferentes estilos, preferencias y habilidades particulares que los ayuden en su aprendizaje. Entre ellos, juegos, proyectos, discusiones, movimientos, dibujos, pantomimas y dramatizaciones. Escoja, en cada unidad, una o más actividades para afianzar el aprendizaje del vocabulario, de manera que haga del mismo una experiencia estimulante, creativa y placentera.

Word by Word intenta ofrecerles a los estudiantes una manera vívida y significativa de practicar el vocabulario inglés. Al expresarle el fin de nuestro programa, esperamos haberle comunicado también su esencia: aprender vocabulario puede estimular una interacción auténtica... puede relacionarse a la experiencia personal de los alumnos... puede ser pertinente a las diferentes habilidades y estilos de aprendizaje de ellos, y... ¡puede ser divertido!

Steven J. Molinsky
Bill Bliss

The *Word by Word* Picture Dictionary presents more than 3,000 vocabulary words through lively full-color illustrations. This innovative Picture Dictionary offers students the essential vocabulary they need to communicate effectively in a wide range of relevant situations and contexts.

Word by Word organizes the vocabulary into 100 thematic units, providing a careful sequence of lessons that range from the immediate world of the student to the world at large. Early units on the family, the home, and daily activities lead to lessons on the community, school, workplace, shopping, recreation, and other topics. *Word by Word* offers extensive coverage of important lifeskill competencies and the vocabulary of school subjects and extracurricular activities. Since each unit is self-contained, *Word by Word* can be used either sequentially or in any desired order.

For users' convenience, the units in *Word by Word* are listed two ways: sequentially in the Table of Contents, and alphabetically in the Thematic Index. These resources, combined with the Glossary in the appendix, allow students and teachers to quickly and easily locate all words and topics in the Picture Dictionary.

The *Word by Word* Picture Dictionary is the centerpiece of the complete *Word by Word* Vocabulary Development Program, which offers a wide selection of print and media support materials for instruction at all levels. Ancillary materials include Workbooks at three different levels (Literacy, Beginning, and Intermediate), a Teacher's Resource Book, a Handbook of Vocabulary Teaching Strategies, a complete Audio Program, Wall Charts, Color Transparencies, Vocabulary Game Cards, a Song Album and accompanying Song Book, and a Testing Program. Bilingual editions of the Picture Dictionary are also available.

Teaching Strategies

Word by Word presents vocabulary words in context. Model conversations depict situations in which people use the words in meaningful communication. These models become the basis for students to engage in dynamic, interactive conversational practice. In addition, writing and discussion questions in each unit encourage students to relate the vocabulary and themes to their own lives as they share experiences, thoughts, opinions, and information about themselves, their cultures, and their countries. In this way, students get to know each other "word by word."

In using *Word by Word*, we encourage you to develop approaches and strategies that are compatible with your own teaching style and the needs and abilities of your students. You may find it helpful to incorporate some of the following techniques for presenting and practicing the vocabulary in each unit.

1. *Previewing the Vocabulary:* Activate students' prior knowledge of the vocabulary either by brainstorming with students the words in the unit they already know and writing them on the board, or by having students look at the Wall Chart, the transparency, or the illustration in *Word by Word* and identify the words they are familiar with.

2. *Presenting the Vocabulary:* Point to the picture of each word, say the word, and have the class repeat it chorally and individually. Check students' understanding and pronunciation of the vocabulary.

3. *Vocabulary Practice:* Have students practice the vocabulary as a class, in pairs, or in small groups. Say or write a word, and have students point to the item or tell the number. Or, point to an item or give the number, and have students say the word.

4. *Model Conversation Practice:* Some units have model conversations that use the first word in the vocabulary list. Other models

are in the form of *skeletal dialogs*, in which vocabulary words can be inserted. (In many skeletal dialogs, bracketed numbers indicate which words can be used to practice the conversation. If no bracketed numbers appear, all the words on the page can be used.)

The following steps are recommended for Model Conversation Practice:

    a. Preview: Students look at the model illustration and discuss who they think the speakers are and where the conversation takes place.

    b. The teacher presents the model and checks students' understanding of the situation and the vocabulary.

    c. Students repeat each line of the conversation chorally or individually.

    d. Students practice the model in pairs.

    e. A pair of students presents a new conversation based on the model, but using a different word from the vocabulary list.

    f. In pairs, students practice several new conversations based on the model, using different vocabulary words.

    g. Pairs present their conversations to the class.

5. *Additional Conversation Practice:* Many units provide two additional skeletal dialogs for further conversation practice with the vocabulary. (These can be found in a yellow-shaded area at the bottom of the page.) Have students practice and present these conversations using any words they wish.

6. *Writing and Spelling Practice:* Have students practice spelling the words as a class, in pairs, or in small groups. Say or spell a word, and have students write it and then point to the picture of the item or tell the number. Or, point to a picture of an item or give the number, and have students write the word.

7. *Themes for Discussion, Composition, Journals, and Portfolios:* Each unit of *Word by Word* provides one or more questions for discussion and composition. (These can be found in a green-shaded area at the bottom of the page.) Have students respond to the questions as a class, in pairs, or in small groups. Or, have students write their responses at home, share their written work with other students, and discuss as a class, in pairs, or in small groups.

Students may enjoy keeping a journal of their written work. If time permits, you may want to write a response in each student's journal, sharing your own opinions and experiences as well as reacting to what the student has written. If you are keeping portfolios of students' work, these compositions serve as excellent examples of students' progress in learning English.

8. *Communication Activities:* The *Word by Word* Teacher's Resource Book provides a wealth of games, tasks, brainstorming, discussion, movement, drawing, miming, role-playing, and other activities designed to take advantage of students' different learning styles and particular abilities and strengths. For each unit, choose one or more of these activities to reinforce students' vocabulary learning in a way that is stimulating, creative, and enjoyable.

Word by Word aims to offer students a communicative, meaningful, and lively way of practicing English vocabulary. In conveying to you the substance of our program, we hope that we have also conveyed the spirit: that learning vocabulary can be genuinely interactive . . . relevant to our students' lives . . . responsive to students' differing strengths and learning styles . . . and fun!

Steven J. Molinsky
Bill Bliss

A. What's your **name**?
B. *Nancy Ann Peterson.*

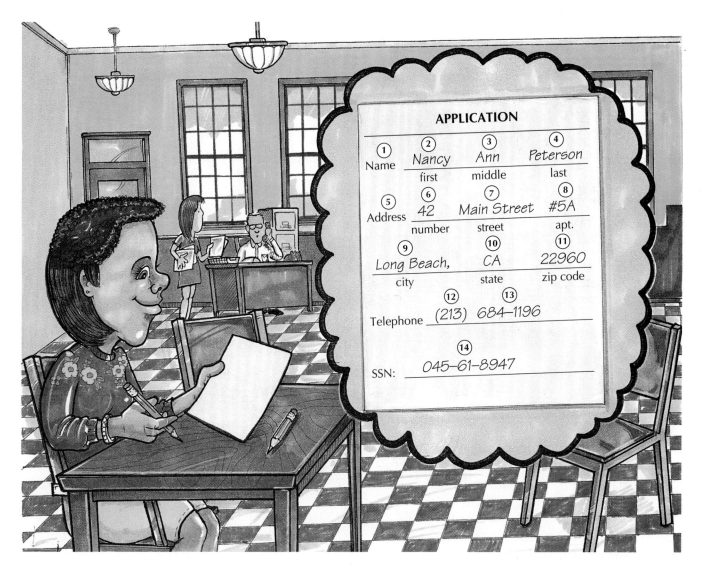

	1. name	nombre completo
nombre(s)	**2.** first name	
otro(s) nombre(s)/ segundo nombre	**3.** middle name	
apellidos (paterno y materno)	**4.** last name/family name/ surname	
dirección	**5.** address	
número de la casa	**6.** street number	
calle	**7.** street	

- nombre completo **1.** name
- nombre(s) **2.** first name
- otro(s) nombre(s)/ segundo nombre **3.** middle name
- apellidos (paterno y materno) **4.** last name/family name/ surname
- dirección **5.** address
- número de la casa **6.** street number
- calle **7.** street

- número del apartamento **8.** apartment number
- ciudad **9.** city
- estado **10.** state
- código/zona postal **11.** zip code
- código telefónico/prefijo telefónico/clave telefónica **12.** area code
- número de teléfono **13.** telephone number/ phone number
- número de seguro social **14.** social security number

A. What's your _____?
B. ....
A. Did you say ....?
B. Yes. That's right.

A. What's your last name?
B. ....
A. How do you spell that?
B. ....

Tell about yourself:
    My name is ....
    My address is ....
    My telephone number is ....
Now interview a friend.

A. Who is she?
B. She's my **wife**.
A. What's her name?
B. Her name is *Betty*.

A. Who is he?
B. He's my **husband**.
A. What's his name?
B. His name is *Fred*.

esposa	**1.** wife	hermano	**8.** brother
esposo	**2.** husband	bebé/nene	**9.** baby
padres	**parents**	abuelos	**grandparents**
madre/mamá	**3.** mother	abuela	**10.** grandmother
padre/papá	**4.** father	abuelo	**11.** grandfather
hijos	**children**	nietos	**grandchildren**
hija	**5.** daughter	nieta	**12.** granddaughter
hijo	**6.** son	nieto	**13.** grandson
hermana	**7.** sister		

A. I'd like to introduce my _____.
B. Nice to meet you.
C. Nice to meet you, too.

A. What's your _____'s name?
B. His/Her name is ....

Tell about your family.
Talk about photos of family
members.

A. Who is she?
B. She's my **aunt**.
A. What's her name?
B. Her name is *Linda*.

A. Who is he?
B. He's my **uncle**.
A. What's his name?
B. His name is *Jack*.

tía	**1.** aunt		suegra	**6.** mother-in-law
tío	**2.** uncle		suegro	**7.** father-in-law
sobrina	**3.** niece		yerno	**8.** son-in-law
sobrino	**4.** nephew		nuera	**9.** daughter-in-law
primo, prima	**5.** cousin		cuñado	**10.** brother-in-law
			cuñada	**11.** sister-in-law

A. Is he/she your _____?
B. No. He's/She's my _____.
A. Oh. What's his/her name?
B. ....

A. Let me introduce my _____.
B. I'm glad to meet you.
C. Nice meeting you, too.

Tell about your relatives:
   What are their names?
   Where do they live?
Draw your family tree and talk
   about it.

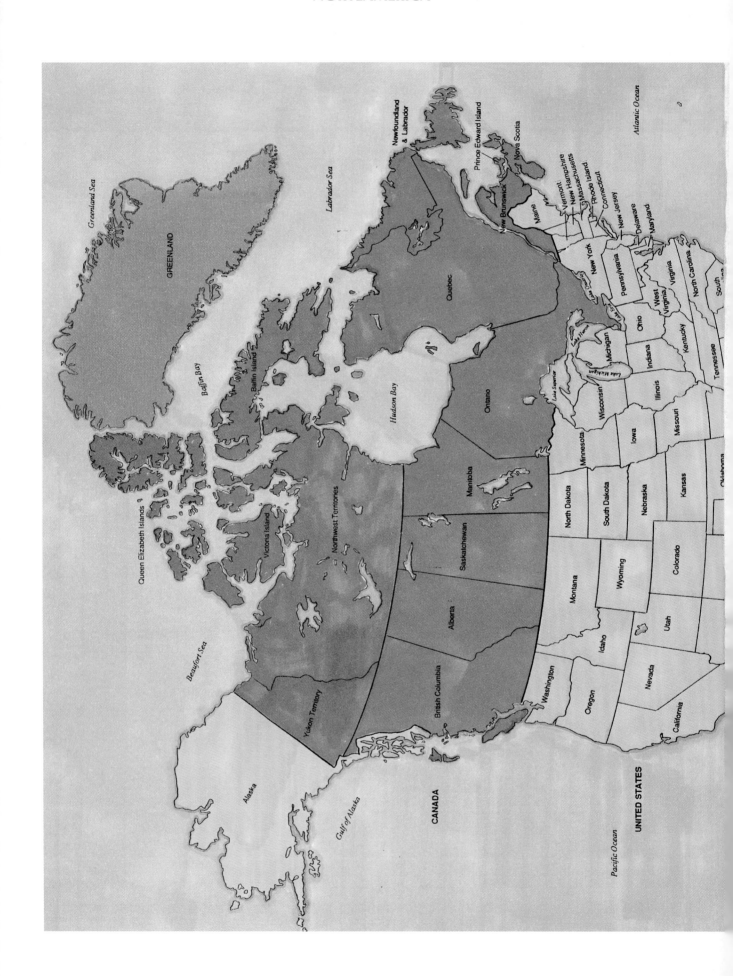

norte **1.** north
sur **2.** south
este **3.** east
oeste **4.** west

noreste **5.** northeast
noroeste **6.** northwest
sureste **7.** southeast
suroeste **8.** southwest

A. Where is ....?

B. .... is ________ of ....

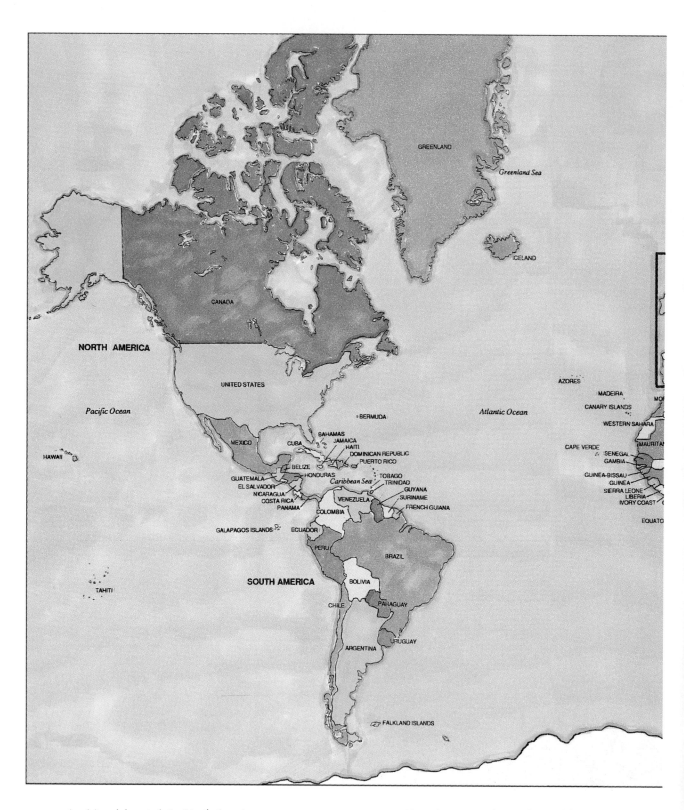

América del norte/ **1.** North America
Norteamérica
América del sur/Suramérica **2.** South America
Europa **3.** Europe
África **4.** Africa

El Medio Oriente/ **5.** The Middle East
El Oriente Medio
Asia **6.** Asia
Australia **7.** Australia
Antártica **8.** Antarctida

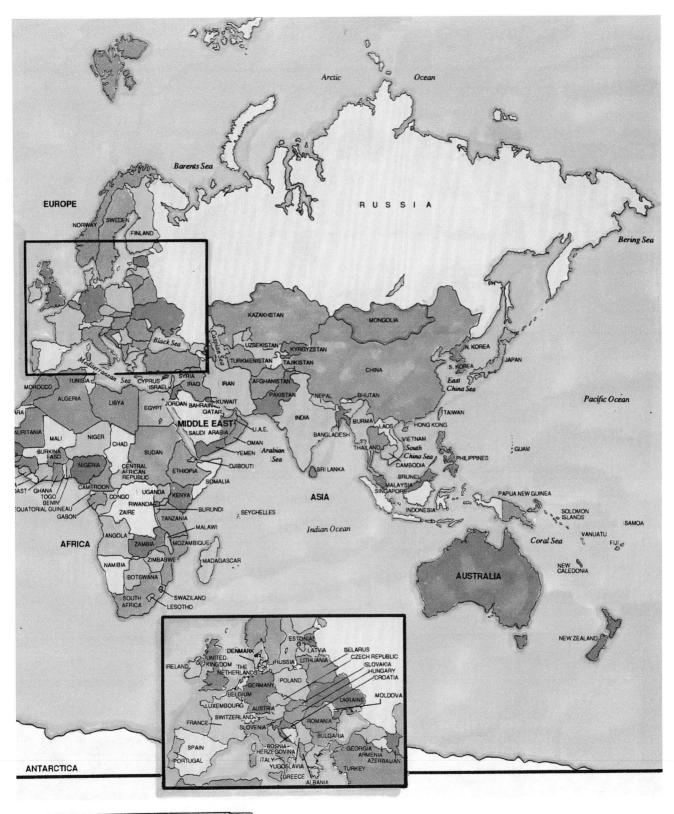

A. Where's ………?

B. It's in _____.

A. What ocean/sea is near ………?

A. What do you do every day?
B. I **get up**, I **take a shower**, and I **brush my teeth**.

levantarse	**1.** get up	hacer la cama	**11.** make the bed
ducharse/bañarse	**2.** take a shower	desvestirse	**12.** get undressed
lavarme los dientes	**3.** brush *my** teeth	bañarse/meterse en la tina	**13.** take a bath
uso la seda dental/	**4.** floss *my** teeth	acostarse	**14.** go to bed
uso el hilo dental		dormir	**15.** sleep
afeitarse	**5.** shave	hacer/preparar el desayuno	**16.** make breakfast
vestirse	**6.** get dressed	hacer/preparar el almuerzo	**17.** make lunch
lavarme la cara	**7.** wash *my** face	hacer/preparar la cena	**18.** cook/make dinner
maquillarse/pintarse	**8.** put on makeup	desayunar	**19.** eat/have breakfast
cepillarme el cabello	**9.** brush *my** hair	almorzar	**20.** eat/have lunch
peinarme el cabello	**10.** comb *my** hair	cenar	**21.** eat/have dinner

*my, his, her, our, your, their

A. What does he do every day?
B. He _____s, he _____s, and he _____s.

A. What does she do every day?
B. She _____s, she _____s, and she _____s.

What do you do every day? Make a list.
Interview some friends and tell about their everyday activities.

A. Hi! What are you doing?
B. I'm **clean**ing **the apartment**.

limpiar el apartamento/ limpiar la casa	**1.**	clean the apartment/ clean the house
barrer	**2.**	sweep the floor
sacudir	**3.**	dust
pasar la aspiradora	**4.**	vacuum
lavar los platos	**5.**	wash the dishes
lavar la ropa	**6.**	do the laundry
aplanchar/planchar	**7.**	iron
darle de comer al bebé/ a la bebé/al nene/a la nena	**8.**	feed the baby
darle de comer al gato	**9.**	feed the cat
pasear al perro	**10.**	walk the dog
ver la televisión/la tele/ el televisor	**11.**	watch TV
oír el radio	**12.**	listen to the radio
escuchar/oír música	**13.**	listen to music
leer	**14.**	read
jugar	**15.**	play
jugar baloncesto/ básquetbol	**16.**	play basketball
tocar la guitarra	**17.**	play the guitar
tocar el piano	**18.**	practice the piano
estudiar	**19.**	study
hacer ejercicios	**20.**	exercise

A. Hi, ...! This is ....
What are you doing?
B. I'm _____ing. How about you?
A. I'm _____ing.

A. Are you going to _____ today?
B. Yes. I'm going to _____ in a little while.

What are you going to do tomorrow?
Make a list of *everything* you are going to do.

A. Where's the **teacher**?
B. The **teacher** is *next to* the **board**.

A. Where's the **pen**?
B. The **pen** is *on* the **desk**.

maestra	**1.** teacher		tiza/gis/pizarrin	**19.** chalk
asistente/auxiliar	**2.** teacher's aide		repisa	**20.** chalk tray
alumno/estudiante	**3.** student		borrador	**21.** eraser
banco/silla	**4.** seat/chair		sistema de altavoz/altoparlante	**22.** P.A. system/loudspeaker
pluma/bolígrafo	**5.** pen		cartelera/tablero/tabilla/mural	**23.** bulletin board
lápiz	**6.** pencil		de anuncios	
borrador/goma de borrar	**7.** eraser		tachuela	**24.** thumbtack
pupitre/escritorio	**8.** desk		mapa	**25.** map
escritorio de la maestra	**9.** teacher's desk		sacapuntas	**26.** pencil sharpener
libro/texto	**10.** book/textbook		globo terráqueo/del mundo	**27.** globe
cuaderno/libreta	**11.** notebook		librera/librero/estante/para	**28.** bookshelf
papel	**12.** notebook paper		libros	
papel cuadriculado	**13.** graph paper		retroproyector	**29.** overhead projector
regla	**14.** ruler		televisor/tele	**30.** TV
calculadora	**15.** calculator		pantalla	**31.** (movie) screen
reloj	**16.** clock		proyector de diapositivas/	**32.** slide projector
bandera	**17.** flag		de transparencias	
pizarra/pizarrón/tablero	**18.** board		computadora	**33.** computer
			proyector de películas	**34.** (movie) projector

A. Is there a/an _____ in your classroom?*
B. Yes. There's a/an _____ next to/on the _____.

A. Is there a/an _____ in your classroom?*
B. No, there isn't.

Describe your classroom.
(There's a/an ....)

*With 12, 13, 19 use: Is there _____ in your classroom?

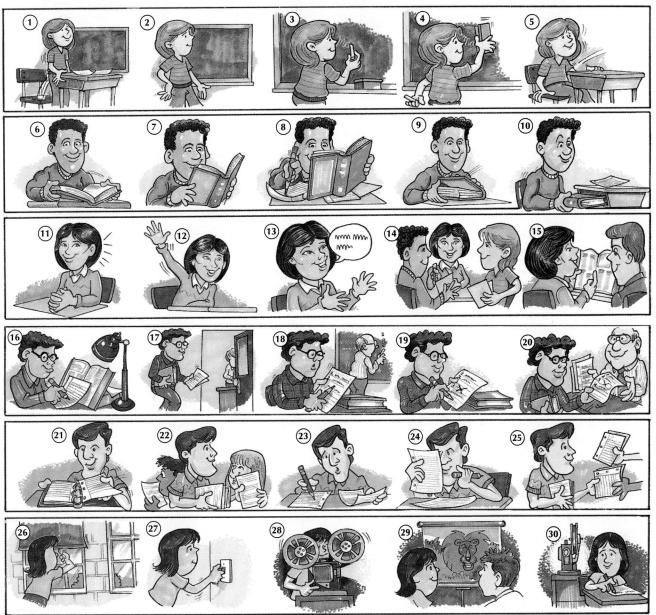

Levánte(n)se.	**1.**	Stand up.
Vaya(n) *al pizarrón/* *a la pizarra/al tablero.*	**2.**	Go to the *board.*
Escriba(n) *su nombre.*	**3.**	Write *your name.*
Borre(n) *su nombre.*	**4.**	Erase *your name.*
Siénte(n)se/Tome(n).	**5.**	Sit down./Take your seat.
Abra(n) *el libro.*	**6.**	Open *your book.*
Lea(n) *la página ocho.*	**7.**	Read *page eight.*
Estudie(n) *la página ocho.*	**8.**	Study *page eight.*
Cierre(n) *el libro.*	**9.**	Close *your book.*
Guarde(n) *el libro.*	**10.**	Put away *your book.*
Escuche(n) *la pregunta.*	**11.**	Listen to *the question.*
Alce(n)/Levante(n) *la mano.*	**12.**	Raise *your hand.*
Conteste(n) *la pregunta.*	**13.**	Give *the answer.*
Trabaje(n) *en grupos.*	**14.**	Work *in groups.*
Ayúdense.	**15.**	Help *each other.*
Haga(n) *su tarea.*	**16.**	Do *your homework.*
Traiga(n) *su tarea.*	**17.**	Bring in *your homework.*

Revise(n) *las respuestas/* *las contestaciones.*	**18.**	Go over *the answers.*
Corrija(n) *sus errores.*	**19.**	Correct *your mistakes.*
Entregue(n) *su tarea.*	**20.**	Hand in *your homework.*
Saque(n) *un papel.*	**21.**	Take out *a piece of paper.*
Pase(n) *el examen/la prueba.*	**22.**	Pass out *the tests.*
Conteste(n) *las preguntas.*	**23.**	Answer *the questions.*
Revise(n) *sus respuestas/* *sus contestaciones.*	**24.**	Check *your answers.*
Recoja(n) *los exámenes/* *las pruebas.*	**25.**	Collect *the tests.*
Baje(n) *las persianas.*	**26.**	Lower *the shades.*
Apague(n) *las luces.*	**27.**	Turn off *the lights.*
Prenda(n)/Ponga(n)/ Enciendan *el proyector.*	**28.**	Turn on *the projector.*
Vea(n) *la película.*	**29.**	Watch *the movie.*
Tome(n) notas	**30.**	Take notes.

You're the teacher! Give instructions to your students.

A. Where are you from?
B. I'm from **Mexico**.

A. What's your nationality?
B. I'm **Mexican**.

A. What language do you speak?
B. I speak **Spanish**.

Country	Nationality	Language	Country	Nationality	Language
Afghanistan	Afghan	Afghan	Italy	Italian	Italian
Argentina	Argentine	Spanish	Japan	Japanese	Japanese
Australia	Australian	English	Jordan	Jordanian	Arabic
Bolivia	Bolivian	Spanish	Korea	Korean	Korean
Brazil	Brazilian	Portuguese	Laos	Laotian	Laotian
Cambodia	Cambodian	Cambodian	Latvia	Latvian	Latvian
Canada	Canadian	English/French	Lithuania	Lithuanian	Lithuanian
Chile	Chilean	Spanish	Malaysia	Malaysian	Malay
China	Chinese	Chinese	Mexico	Mexican	Spanish
Colombia	Colombian	Spanish	New Zealand	New Zealander	English
Costa Rica	Costa Rican	Spanish	Nicaragua	Nicaraguan	Spanish
Cuba	Cuban	Spanish	Panama	Panamanian	Spanish
(The) Dominican Republic	Dominican	Spanish	Peru	Peruvian	Spanish
Ecuador	Ecuadorian	Spanish	(The) Philippines	Filipino	Tagalog
Egypt	Egyptian	Arabic	Poland	Polish	Polish
El Salvador	Salvadorean	Spanish	Portugal	Portuguese	Portuguese
England	English	English	Puerto Rico	Puerto Rican	Spanish
Estonia	Estonian	Estonian	Romania	Romanian	Romanian
Ethiopia	Ethiopian	Amharic	Russia	Russian	Russian
France	French	French	Saudi Arabia	Saudi	Arabic
Germany	German	German	Spain	Spanish	Spanish
Greece	Greek	Greek	Taiwan	Taiwanese	Chinese
Guatemala	Guatemalan	Spanish	Thailand	Thai	Thai
Haiti	Haitian	Haitian Kreyol	Turkey	Turkish	Turkish
Honduras	Honduran	Spanish	Ukraine	Ukrainian	Ukrainian
Indonesia	Indonesian	Indonesian	(The) United States	American	English
Israel	Israeli	Hebrew	Venezuela	Venezuelan	Spanish
			Vietnam	Vietnamese	Vietnamese

A. What's your native language?
B. _____.
A. Oh. What country are you from?
B. _____.

A. Where are you and your husband/wife going on your vacation?
B. We're going to _____.
A. That's nice. Tell me, do you speak _____?
B. No, but my husband/wife does. He's/She's _____.

Tell about yourself:
Where are you from?
What's your nationality?
What languages do you speak?
Now interview and tell about a friend.

A. Where do you live?
B. I live in an **apartment building**.

edificio de apartamentos	**1.** apartment (building)
casa	**2.** (single-family) house
duplex/casas de dos plantas	**3.** duplex/two-family house
adosadas en pares	
casas en hileras/de dos o tres	**4.** townhouse/townhome
plantas en hileras	
condominio/condo/piso	**5.** condominium/condo
dormitorio/	**6.** dormitory/dorm
residencia estudiantil	

caraván/casa móvil/	**7.** mobile home/trailer
casa rodante/trailer	
hacienda/granja/finca	**8.** farmhouse
cabaña	**9.** cabin
asilo/casa de ancianos/	**10.** nursing home
de reposo/para personas	
de la tercera edad	
refugio/albergue/asilo	**11.** shelter
para pobres	
casa flotante	**12.** houseboat

A. Town Taxi Company.
B. Hello. Please send a taxi to
   (address) .
A. Is that a house or an apartment?
B. It's a/an _____.
A. All right. We'll be there right
   away.

A. This is the Emergency Operator.
B. Please send an ambulance to
   (address) .
A. Is that a private home?
B. It's a/an _____.
A. What's your name?
B. ....
A. And your telephone number?
B. ....

Tell about people you know and the
types of housing they live in.
Discuss:
   Who lives in dormitories?
   Who lives in nursing homes?
   Who lives in shelters?
   Why?

LA SALA

A. Where are you?
B. I'm in the living room.
A. What are you doing?
B. I'm *dusting** the **coffee table**.

*dusting/cleaning

mesa de centro	**1.** coffee table	
alfombra	**2.** rug	
piso	**3.** floor	
sillón/silla de brazos/butaca	**4.** armchair	
mesita/esquinera/mesilla	**5.** end table	
lámpara/lámpara de mesa	**6.** lamp	
pantalla	**7.** lampshade	
ventana	**8.** window	
cortinas	**9.** drapes/curtains	
sofá	**10.** sofa/couch	
cojín	**11.** (throw) pillow	
cielo raso	**12.** ceiling	
pared	**13.** wall	
mueble/mueble de pared/ unidad de módulos/ centro de entretenimiento	**14.** wall unit/entertainment unit	
televisor	**15.** television	
videograbadora/ videoreproductora	**16.** video cassette recorder/VCR	
estéreo/equipo estereofónico	**17.** stereo system	
bocina	**18.** speaker	
canapé/sofá pequeño	**19.** loveseat	
mata/planta	**20.** plant	
cuadro	**21.** painting	
marco	**22.** frame	
repisa	**23.** mantel	
hogar/chimenea	**24.** fireplace	
rejilla (para la chimenea)	**25.** fireplace screen	
foto/fotografía/retrato	**26.** picture/photograph	
librera/librero/ estante para libros	**27.** bookcase	

A. You have a lovely living room!
B. Oh, thank you.
A. Your _____ is/are beautiful!
B. Thank you for saying so.

A. Uh-oh! I just spilled coffee on your _____!
B. That's okay. Don't worry about it.

Tell about your living room.
(In my living room there's ....)

A. This **dining room table** is very nice.
B. Thank you. It was a gift from my *grandmother.**

*grandmother/grandfather/aunt/uncle/...

mesa de comedor	**1.** (dining room) table	mantel	**11.** tablecloth
silla/silla de comedor	**2.** (dining room) chair	candelero	**12.** candlestick
vitrina/chinero/	**3.** china cabinet	vela	**13.** candle
alacena para la loza		centro de mesa	**14.** centerpiece
vajilla/vajilla de porcelana/	**4.** china	salero	**15.** salt shaker
vajilla de loza		pimentero	**16.** pepper shaker
lámpara de araña/de techo/	**5.** chandelier	mantequillera	**17.** butter dish
candil de techo		carrito de servir	**18.** serving cart
aparador	**6.** buffet	tetera	**19.** teapot
ensaladera	**7.** salad bowl	cafetera	**20.** coffee pot
jarra	**8.** pitcher	jarrita para la leche/	**21.** creamer
fuente honda/sopera	**9.** serving bowl	para la crema/lechera/cremera	
bandeja	**10.** serving platter	azucarera	**22.** sugar bowl

[In a store]

A. May I help you?
B. Yes, please. Do you have
   _____s?*
A. Yes. _____s* are right over there.
B. Thank you.

*With 4, use the singular.

[At home]

A. Look at this old _____
   I just bought!
B. Where did you buy it?
A. At a yard sale. How do you
   like it?
B. It's VERY unusual!

Tell about your dining room.
(In my dining room there's ....)

EL COMEDOR: UN CUBIERTO/UN PUESTO

A. Excuse me. Where does the **salad plate** go?
B. It goes *to the left of* the **dinner plate**.

A. Excuse me. Where does the **soup spoon** go?
B. It goes *to the right of* the **teaspoon**.

A. Excuse me. Where does the **wine glass** go?
B. It goes *between* the **water glass** and the
cup and saucer.

A. Excuse me. Where does the **cup** go?
B. It goes *on* the **saucer**.

plato para la ensalada	**1.** salad plate	**vajilla de plata/vajilla de**	**silverware**
platito para el pan y	**2.** bread-and-butter plate	**cubiertos/juego de cubiertos**	
la mantequilla		tenedor para la ensalada/	**10.** salad fork
plato	**3.** dinner plate	para el primer plato	
plato para la sopa/plato hondo	**4.** soup bowl	tenedor/trinche	**11.** dinner fork
vaso	**5.** water glass	cuchillo	**12.** knife
copa	**6.** wine glass	cucharita/cucharilla	**13.** teaspoon
taza	**7.** cup	cuchara	**14.** soup spoon
platito/platillo	**8.** saucer	cuchillo para la mantequilla	**15.** butter knife
servilleta	**9.** napkin		

A. Waiter? Excuse me. This
_____ is dirty.
B. I'm terribly sorry. I'll get you
another _____ right away.

A. Oops! I dropped my _____!
B. That's okay! I'll get you another
_____ from the kitchen.

Practice giving directions. Tell
someone how to set a table.
(Put the ....)

LA RECÁMARA/EL DORMITORIO

A. Ooh! Look at that big bug!!
B. Where?
A. It's on the **bed**!
B. I'LL get it.

cama	**1.**	bed
cabecera	**2.**	headboard
almohada	**3.**	pillow
funda	**4.**	pillowcase
sábana/sábana ceñida para el cochón	**5.**	fitted sheet
sábana/sábana para arroparse	**6.**	(flat) sheet
manta/cobija/frisa	**7.**	blanket
manta eléctrica/frisa eléctrica	**8.**	electric blanket
volante/pollera	**9.**	dust ruffle
sobrecama/cubrecama/colcha/frazada	**10.**	bedspread
edredón	**11.**	comforter/quilt
pie de la cama	**12.**	footboard
persianas	**13.**	blinds
mesita de noche	**14.**	night table/nightstand
despertador	**15.**	alarm clock
radio reloj/despertador	**16.**	clock radio
ropero/gavetero/gavetera/chifonier	**17.**	chest (of drawers)

espejo	**18.**	mirror
joyero	**19.**	jewelry box
cómoda/tocador/chiforobe	**20.**	dresser/bureau
cama gemela/sencilla/individual	**21.**	twin bed
colchón	**22.**	mattress
colchón de muelles	**23.**	box spring
cama doble/camera	**24.**	double bed
cama de matrimonio/doble/doble cama	**25.**	queen-size bed
cama tamaño king/cama gigante	**26.**	king-size bed
cama litera/cama camarote	**27.**	bunk bed
cama nido	**28.**	trundle bed
sofá cama	**29.**	sofa bed/convertible sofa
canapé	**30.**	day bed
catre	**31.**	cot
cama con colchón de agua	**32.**	water bed
cama con baldaquín(o)/con dosel/con tolda	**33.**	canopy bed
cama de hospital	**34.**	hospital bed

[In a store]

A. Excuse me. I'm looking for a/an _____.*
B. We have some very nice _____s. And they're all on sale this week.
A. Oh, good!

*With 13, use: Excuse me. I'm looking for _____.

[In a bedroom]

A. Oh, no! I just lost my contact lens!
B. Where?
A. I think it's on the _____.
B. I'll help you look.

Tell about your bedroom.
(In my bedroom there's ....)

A. I think we need a new **dishwasher**.
B. I think you're right.

lavaplatos/lavadora de platos/ máquina de lavar platos/lavavajillas	**1.** dishwasher	
jabón para la lavadora de platos	**2.** dishwasher detergent	
jabón liquido para lavar platos	**3.** dishwashing liquid	
grifo/pluma/llave	**4.** faucet	
fregador/fregadero	**5.** (kitchen) sink	
triturador de desperdicios	**6.** (garbage) disposal	
esponja	**7.** sponge	
estropajo/brillo	**8.** scouring pad	
cepillo para restregar ollas	**9.** pot scrubber	
escurridero/escurreplatos	**10.** dish rack	
colgador para papel de toalla	**11.** paper towel holder	
trapo/paño/toalla de cocina/limpión	**12.** dish towel	
compresor de basura	**13.** trash compactor	
gabinete	**14.** cabinet	
horno microondas	**15.** microwave (oven)	
mostrador	**16.** (kitchen) counter	
tablita/tabla para picar/picador	**17.** cutting board	

latas/envases para harina, azúcar, té o sal	**18.** canister	
estufa/cocina/hornillo	**19.** stove/range	
quemador/fogón/hornillo/hornilla	**20.** burner	
horno	**21.** oven	
agarrador de ollas	**22.** potholder	
tostadora	**23.** toaster	
tablilla para especias/especiero	**24.** spice rack	
abridor de latas/abrelatas eléctrico	**25.** (electric) can opener	
libro de recetas de cocina	**26.** cookbook	
refrigerador/refrigeradora/nevera	**27.** refrigerator	
congelador	**28.** freezer	
dispensador de hielo automático	**29.** ice maker	
bandeja/gavetao/cubeta de hielo	**30.** ice tray	
plaquita/chapita magnética	**31.** refrigerator magnet	
mesa	**32.** kitchen table	
individual/mantelito individual	**33.** placemat	
silla	**34.** kitchen chair	
cubo/bote de basura/basurero/ tinaco/zafacón	**35.** garbage pail	

[In a store]
A. Excuse me. Are your _____s still on sale?
B. Yes, they are. They're twenty percent off.

[In a kitchen]
A. When did you get this/these new _____(s)?
B. I got it/them last week.

Tell about your kitchen.
(In my kitchen there's …………)

A. Could I possibly borrow your **wok**?
B. Sure. I'll get it for you right now.
A. Thanks.

disco chino/wok	**1.** wok	batidora eléctrica/mezcladora eléctrica	**23.** (electric) mixer
olla/caldera/cazo	**2.** pot	procesador de alimentos	**24.** food processor
cacerola	**3.** saucepan	sartén eléctrico	**25.** electric frying pan
tapadera/tapa	**4.** lid/cover/top	máquina de hacer barquillos o waffles/	**26.** waffle iron
sartén	**5.** frying pan/skillet	wafflera	
bandeja de asar/de hornear	**6.** roasting pan	plancha eléctrica	**27.** (electric) griddle
cazuela/olla para asar	**7.** roaster	máquina de hacer rosetas/palomitas/	**28.** popcorn maker
baño de María	**8.** double boiler	rositas/hojuelas de maíz	
olla de presión	**9.** pressure cooker	licuadora eléctrica	**29.** blender
colador	**10.** colander	rallo/rallador	**30.** grater
cazuela	**11.** casserole (dish)	batidor de mano	**31.** (egg) beater
molde para bizcochos	**12.** cake pan	cucharón	**32.** ladle
/para pasteles/para tartas/tortera/tartera	**13.** pie plate	cuchara de helados	**33.** ice cream scoop
plancha para hornear galletas	**14.** cookie sheet	molde de hacer galletas	**34.** cookie cutter
tazón/cuenco	**15.** (mixing) bowl	colador	**35.** strainer
rodillo/rolo	**16.** rolling pin	triturador/machacador de ajos	**36.** garlic press
taza de medir	**17.** measuring cup	abrebotellas/abridor de botellas	**37.** bottle opener
cuchara de medir	**18.** measuring spoon	abrelatas/abridor de latas	**38.** can opener
cafetera	**19.** coffeemaker	batidor de mano	**39.** whisk
molinillo	**20.** coffee grinder	mondador/pelador de vegetales/de papas	**40.** (vegetable) peeler
hervidor/tacho para calentar/hervir agua	**21.** tea kettle	cuchillo	**41.** knife
tostador/tostadora/hornito/horno pastelero	**22.** toaster oven	espátula	**42.** spatula
		mondador	**43.** paring knife

A. What are you looking for?
B. I'm looking for the _____.*
A. Did you look in the drawers/
in the cabinets/next to the
_____/…………?
B. Yes. I looked everywhere!

*With 2, 4, 12–15, 41, use:
I'm looking for a _____.

[A Commercial]
Come to *Kitchen World*! We have
everything you need for your kitchen,
from _____s and _____s, to
_____s and _____s. Are you
looking for a new _____? Is it time
to throw out your old _____? Come
to *Kitchen World* today! We have
everything you need!

What things do you have in your
kitchen?
Which things do you use very often?
Which things do you rarely use?

A. Thank you for the **teddy bear.** It's a very nice gift.
B. You're welcome. Tell me, when are you due?
A. In a few more weeks.

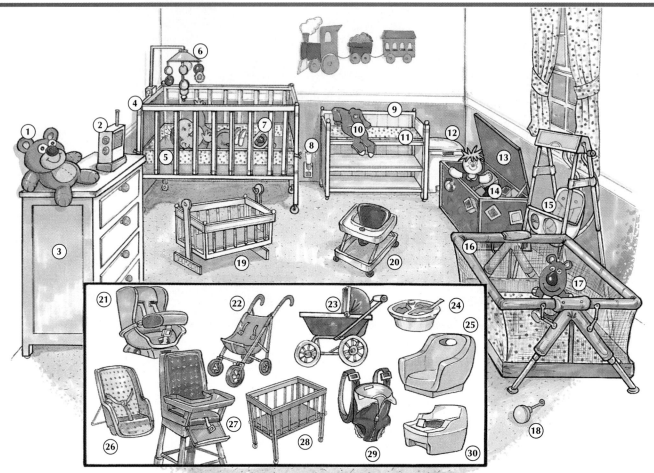

peluche/osito de peluche	**1.** teddy bear	corral	**16.** playpen
intercomunicador	**2.** intercom	peluche/muñeco/	**17.** stuffed animal
gavetero/gavetera/ropero	**3.** chest (of drawers)	muñeca de trapo	
cuna	**4.** crib	sonajero/sonajera/	**18.** rattle
banda protectora/orillero/	**5.** crib bumper	sonaja/maraquita	
paragolpes de cuna		cuna/cuna mecedora	**19.** cradle
móvil	**6.** mobile	andadera/pollera/anador	**20.** walker
juguete de cuna	**7.** crib toy	asiento/portabebé/moisés	**21.** car seat
lamparita/lamparilla/lucecita	**8.** night light	carrito/carriola/coche	**22.** stroller
camilla/mesa para cambiar pañales	**9.** changing table/	coche/cochecito/carricoche	**23.** baby carriage
	dressing table	plato térmico/termo para bebés	**24.** food warmer
pelele elástico/pijamita elástica	**10.** stretch suit	sillita elevadora	**25.** booster seat
colchoneta/almohadilla para	**11.** changing pad	sillita de infante/	**26.** baby seat
la mesa de cambiar pañales		portabebé/moisés	
cubo/bote/zafacón para pañales	**12.** diaper pail	trona/silla alta para bebés	**27.** high chair
baúl para juguetes	**13.** toy chest	cuna portátil	**28.** portable crib
muñeca	**14.** doll	portabebé	**29.** baby carrier
columpio	**15.** swing	bacinilla/bacenilla/bacín	**30.** potty

A. That's a very nice _____.
   Where did you get it?
B. It was a gift from ....

A. Do you have everything you
   need before the baby comes?
B. Almost everything. We're still
   looking for a/an _____ and
   a/an _____.

Tell about your country:
   What things do people buy for a
   new baby?
   Does a new baby sleep in a separate
   room, as in the United States?

EL CUIDADO DEL BEBÉ

[1–12]
A. Do we need anything from the store?
B. Yes. Could you get some more **baby powder**?
A. Sure.

[13–17]
A. Do we need anything from the store?
B. Yes. Could you get another **pacifier**?
A. Sure.

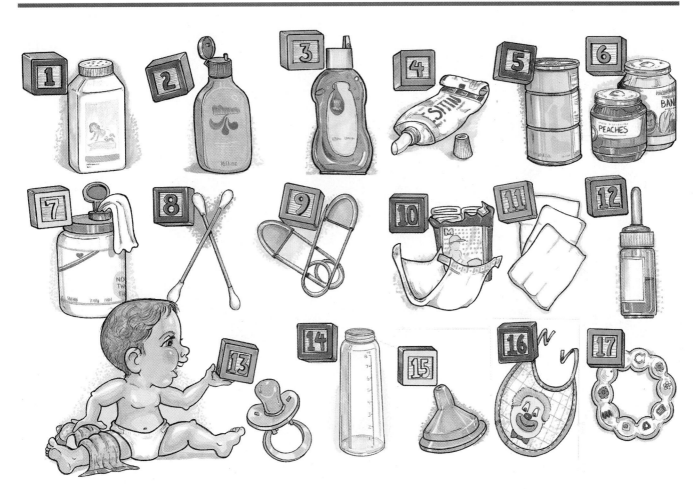

polvo/talco para niños	**1.** baby powder	pañales desechables	**10.** disposable diapers
loción para niños	**2.** baby lotion	pañales de tela/	**11.** cloth diapers
champú para niños	**3.** baby shampoo	de algodón	
ungüento	**4.** ointment	vitaminas en líquido/	**12.** (liquid) vitamins
fórmula	**5.** formula	vitaminas en gotas	
papillas/alimentos para niños/colados	**6.** baby food	chupón/chupete/chupador/	**13.** pacifier
servilletas /toallitas desechables	**7.** (baby) wipes	consuelo/bobo	
palitos/palillos de algodón/	**8.** cotton swabs	mamadera/biberón/tetero	**14.** bottle
hisopos/hisopillos		mamadera/tetina/tetilla	**15.** nipple
alfileres/imperdibles	**9.** diaper pins	babero	**16.** bib
		chupador	**17.** teething ring

[In a store]
A. Excuse me. I can't find the _____.*
B. I'm sorry. We're out of _____.* We'll have some more tomorrow.

[At home]
A. Honey? Where did you put the _____?
B. It's/They're in/on/next to the _____.

In your opinion, which are better: cloth diapers or disposable diapers? Why?
Tell about baby products in your country.

*With 13–17, use the plural.

A. Where's the **plunger**?
B. It's *next to* the **toilet**.

A. Where's the **toothbrush**?
B. It's *in* the **toothbrush holder**.

A. Where's the **washcloth**?
B. It's *on* the **towel rack**.

A. Where's the **mirror**?
B. It's *over* the **sink**.

bomba destapacaños/desatascador	**1.** plunger
inodoro/taza de escusado/tazón/retrete	**2.** toilet
tanque/cisterna	**3.** toilet tank
redondela/silla/asiento del inodoro	**4.** toilet seat
desodorante/desodorizador/ aromatizante ambiental	**5.** air freshener
rodillo del papel higiénico	**6.** toilet paper holder
papel higiénico	**7.** toilet paper
cepillo	**8.** toilet brush
barra para la toalla/colgador de toallas/toallero	**9.** towel rack
toalla (de bano)	**10.** bath towel
toalla para las manos	**11.** hand towel
toallita para la cara	**12.** washcloth/facecloth
canasta/cesto para la ropa sucia	**13.** hamper
pesa	**14.** (bathroom) scale
repisa/tablilla	**15.** shelf
secadora de cabello/de pelo	**16.** hair dryer
ventilador/abanico eléctrico	**17.** fan
espejo	**18.** mirror
botiquín/gabinete	**19.** medicine cabinet/ medicine chest
lavabo/lavamanos	**20.** (bathroom) sink

llave/pluma de agua caliente	**21.** hot water faucet
llave/pluma de agua fría	**22.** cold water faucet
vaso	**23.** cup
cepillo de dientes	**24.** toothbrush
colgador de cepillos de dientes/portacepillos	**25.** toothbrush holder
jabón	**26.** soap
jabonera	**27.** soap dish
dispensador de jabón	**28.** soap dispenser
sistema de higiene dental a presión de agua	**29.** Water Pik
gabinete/mueble	**30.** vanity
cesto/canasta para la basura	**31.** wastebasket
regadera/ducha/baño	**32.** shower
barra para la cortina de baño	**33.** shower curtain rod
regadera/ducha	**34.** shower head
anillos/sujetadores/ aros para la cortina de baño	**35.** shower curtain rings
cortina de baño	**36.** shower curtain
tina/bañera	**37.** bathtub/tub
desagüe/escurridor	**38.** drain
parche antirresbalón/alfombrilla/ estera de goma	**39.** rubber mat
esponja	**40.** sponge
alfombra de baño	**41.** bath mat/bath rug

A. [Knock. Knock.] Did I leave my glasses in there?
B. Yes. They're on/in/next to the _____.

A. *Bobby?*
B. Yes, Mom/Dad?
A. You didn't clean up the bathroom! There's toothpaste on the _____ and there's powder all over the _____!
B. Sorry, Mom/Dad. I'll clean it up right away.

Tell about your bathroom.
(In my bathroom there's ....)

ARTÍCULOS DE TOCADOR Y COSMÉTICOS

[1–17]
A. Excuse me. Where can I find **toothbrush**es?
B. They're in the next aisle.
A. Thank you.

[18–38]
A. Excuse me. Where can I find **shampoo**?
B. It's in the next aisle.
A. Thank you.

cepillo de dientes	1. toothbrush
peine/peinilla	2. comb
cepillo para el cabello/el pelo	3. (hair) brush
máquina de afeitar/de rasurar	4. razor
navaja	5. razor blades
máquina de afeitar/	6. electric razor/
de rasurar eléctrica	electric shaver
astringente	7. styptic pencil
gorra(o) de baño	8. shower cap
lima de metal para las uñas	9. nail file
lima de cartón para las uñas	10. emery board
cortauñas	11. nail clipper
cepillo de uñas	12. nail brush
tijeras	13. scissors
pinzas de sacar cejas	14. tweezers
ganchos para el cabello	15. bobby pins
horquillas para el cabello/	16. hair clips
sujetadores de cabello/pelo	
pasadores/hebillas de cabello	17. barrettes
champú	18. shampoo
enjuage/acondicionador	19. conditioner/rinse

fijador para el cabello	20. hairspray
pasta de dientes/crema dental	21. toothpaste
antiséptico/enjuague bucal	22. mouthwash
seda/hilo dental/hilo de dientes	23. dental floss
crema para afeitarse/para rasurarse/de afeitar	24. shaving creme
crema refrescante	25. after shave lotion
deodorante/desodorante	26. deodorant
talco/polvo	27. powder
crema/loción para las manos	28. hand lotion
perfume/colonia	29. perfume/cologne
betún/pasta lustradora para zapatos	30. shoe polish
esmalte de uñas	31. nail polish
acetona/quitaesmalte de uñas	32. nail polish remover
maquillaje	**makeup**
base para el maquillaje	33. base/foundation
colorete	34. blush/rouge
lápiz de labio/carmín	35. lipstick
sombra para los ojos	36. eye shadow
lápiz delineador/delineador de ojos	37. eye liner
rimel/pintador de pestañas	38. mascara

A. I'm going to the drug store to get a/an _____.*
B. While you're there, could you also get a/an _____?*
A. Sure.

*With 5, 13–38, use: get _____.

A. Do you have everything for the trip?
B. I think so.
A. Did you remember to pack your _____?
B. Oops! I forgot. Thanks for reminding me.

You're going on a trip. Make a list of personal care products you need to take with you.

[1–17, 28–39]

A. Excuse me. Do you sell **broom**s?
B. Yes. They're at the back of the store.
A. Thanks.

[18–27]

A. Excuse me. Do you sell **laundry detergent**?
B. Yes. It's at the back of the store.
A. Thanks.

escoba	**1.** broom	almidón	**21.** starch
recogedor	**2.** dustpan	quitaestática	**22.** static cling remover
escobilla	**3.** whisk broom	farola/limpiador en polvo	**23.** cleanser
plumero/sacudidor	**4.** feather duster	líquido para limpiar ventanas	**24.** window cleaner
limpión/trapo para limpiar	**5.** dust cloth	amoniaco/amoníaco	**25.** ammonia
plancha	**6.** iron	cera para muebles	**26.** furniture polish
tabla de (a)planchar	**7.** ironing board	cera para el piso	**27.** floor wax
barredor de alfombra	**8.** carpet sweeper	papel toalla/papel absorbente	**28.** paper towels
aspiradora	**9.** vacuum (cleaner)	gancho de colgar/colgador de ropa/	**29.** hanger
accesorios para la aspiradora	**10.** vacuum cleaner attachments	hombreras	
bolsa para la aspiradora	**11.** vacuum cleaner bag	canasta para la ropa sucia	**30.** laundry basket
aspiradora de mano/aspiradora portátil	**12.** hand vacuum	bolsa para la ropa sucia	**31.** laundry bag
trapeador	**13.** (dust) mop/(dry) mop	tina para lavar	**32.** utility sink
trapeador de esponja	**14.** (sponge) mop	cepillo para limpiar el inodoro	**33.** scrub brush
trapeador/fregona	**15.** (wet) mop	esponja	**34.** sponge
lavadora	**16.** washing machine/washer	cubo/cubeta	**35.** bucket/pail
secadora	**17.** dryer	basurero/bote para basura/	**36.** trash can/garbage can
detergente	**18.** laundry detergent	tinaco/zafacón	
enjuage/suavizador	**19.** fabric softener	caja para artículos renovables/reciclables	**37.** recycling bin
blanqueador	**20.** bleach	cordón/cuerda/soga para tender ropa	**38.** clothesline
		horquillas/pinzas/pinches/	**39.** clothespins
		ganchos para tender ropa	

A. How do you like this/these
    _____?
B. It's/They're great!

A. They're having a big sale at Dave's Discount Store this week.
B. Oh, really? What's on sale?
A. __[18–27]__ and __[1–17, 28–39]__ s.

Who does the cleaning and laundry in your home? What things does that person use?

A. When are you going to repair the **lamppost**?
B. I'm going to repair it next Saturday.

farol	**1.** lamppost	entrada para el coche/para el carro	**18.** driveway
casilla/casillero postal	**2.** mailbox	desagüe/gotera	**19.** gutter
entrada	**3.** front walk	desagüe/caño	**20.** drainpipe/downspout
escalinatas	**4.** front steps		
porche/portal	**5.** (front) porch	plataforma/terraza/asoleadera	**21.** deck
contrapuerta	**6.** storm door	puerta de atrás	**22.** back door
puerta principal	**7.** front door	agarrador/tirador/perilla	**23.** doorknob
timbre	**8.** doorbell	puerta con tela metálica	**24.** screen door
luz de la entrada	**9.** (front) light	puerta lateral	**25.** side door
ventana	**10.** window	antena parabólica	**26.** satellite dish
malla/tela metálica	**11.** (window) screen	patio	**27.** patio
contraventana/postigo	**12.** shutter	cortacésped/cortagrama/máquina cortadora de césped/de grama/de zacate	**28.** lawnmower
tejado/techo	**13.** roof		
antena de televisión	**14.** TV antenna	barbacoa/parrilla	**29.** barbecue/(outdoor) grill
chimenea	**15.** chimney		
garaje/estacionamiento/cochera	**16.** garage	silla de jardín	**30.** lawn chair
puerta del garaje/puerta del estacionamiento/puerta de la cochera	**17.** garage door	barraca/caseta para herramientas	**31.** tool shed

[On the telephone]
A. Harry's Home Repairs.
B. Hello. Do you fix _____s?
A. No, we don't.
B. Oh, okay. Thank you.

[At work on Monday morning]
A. What did you do this weekend?
B. Nothing much. I repaired my _____ and my _____.

Do you like to repair things?
What things can you repair yourself?
What things can't you repair? Who repairs them?

EL EDIFICIO DE APARTAMENTOS

A. Is there a **lobby**?
B. Yes, there is. Do you want to see the apartment?
A. Yes, I do.

vestíbulo	**1.**	lobby
portero automático/eléctrico	**2.**	intercom
timbre/zumbador/chicharra	**3.**	buzzer
casillero postal	**4.**	mailbox
ascensor/elevador	**5.**	elevator
portero	**6.**	doorman
detector de humo	**7.**	smoke detector
mirilla	**8.**	peephole
cadena antirrobo/ de seguridad	**9.**	(door) chain
cerradura con pestillo	**10.**	dead-bolt lock
aire acondicionado	**11.**	air conditioner

alarma contra incendios	**12.**	fire alarm
disparador/shuta de basura/rampa/escape/ conducto para la basura	**13.**	garbage chute
lavandería	**14.**	laundry room
supervisor/super	**15.**	superintendent
depósito	**16.**	storage room
garaje/estacionamiento con techo	**17.**	parking garage
estacionamiento	**18.**	parking lot
balcón/terraza	**19.**	balcony/terrace
piscina/alberca/pileta	**20.**	swimming pool
bañera de hidromasaje de terapia/tina de terapia/tina-jacuzzi	**21.**	whirlpool

[Renting an apartment]

A. Let me show you around the building.*
B. Okay.
A. This is the _____ and here's the _____.
B. I see.

*With 7–11, use:
　Let me show you around the apartment.

[On the telephone]

A. Mom and Dad? I found an apartment.
B. Good. Tell us about it.
A. It has a/an _____ and a/an _____.
B. That's nice. Does it have a/an _____?
A. Yes, it does.

Tell about the differences between living in a house and in an apartment building.

A. Did you remember to pay the **carpenter**?
B. Yes. I wrote a check yesterday.

carpintero	**1.** carpenter	la cuenta del gas	**12.** gas bill
ayudante	**2.** handyman	la cuenta de la electricidad	**13.** electric bill
pintor	**3.** (house) painter	la cuenta del teléfono	**14.** telephone bill
deshollinador	**4.** chimney sweep	la cuenta del agua	**15.** water bill
reparador de electrodomésticos/	**5.** appliance repair person	la cuenta de la calefacción	**16.** oil bill/heating bill
de artefactos eléctricos		la cuenta del cable	**17.** cable TV bill
reparador de televisión	**6.** TV repair person	la cuenta de la fumigación	**18.** pest control bill
cerrajero	**7.** locksmith	alquiler	**19.** rent
jardinero	**8.** gardener	mensualidad/cuota para el	**20.** parking fee
electricista	**9.** electrician	estacionamiento	
plomero	**10.** plumber	hipoteca	**21.** mortgage payment
fumigador	**11.** exterminator		

[1–11]
A. When is the _____ going to come?
B. This afternoon.

[12–21]
A. When is the _____ due?
B. It's due at the end of the month.

Tell about utilities, services, and repairs you pay for. How much do you pay?

HERRAMIENTAS

A. Could I borrow your **hammer***?
B. Sure.
A. Thanks.

With 28–32, use: Could I borrow some _____s?

martillo	**1.** hammer		sierra eléctrica	**17.** power saw
destornillador	**2.** screwdriver		nivel/prensa	**18.** level
destornillador/de estrías/Phillips	**3.** Phillips screwdriver		cepillo de carpintero/ garlopa	**19.** plane
llave inglesa/para tuercas	**4.** wrench		caja de herramientas	**20.** toolbox
alicates/pinzas	**5.** pliers		bandeja para la pintura	**21.** (paint) pan
sierra/serrucho	**6.** hacksaw		rodillo	**22.** (paint) roller
hacha	**7.** hatchet		brocha	**23.** paintbrush/brush
llave inglesa	**8.** monkey wrench		pintura	**24.** paint
serrucho	**9.** saw		trementina/aguarrás/terpina	**25.** paint thinner
taladro de mano/taladradora	**10.** hand drill		lija	**26.** sandpaper
berbiquí/soporte para taladro de mano	**11.** brace		alambre	**27.** wire
cincel	**12.** chisel		clavo	**28.** nail
raspador/espátula	**13.** scraper		tornillo	**29.** screw
torno/tornillo/prensa de banco	**14.** vise		arandela	**30.** washer
barrena/taladro eléctrico	**15.** electric drill		perno	**31.** bolt
broca	**16.** (drill) bit		tuerca	**32.** nut

[1–4, 6–27]
A. Where's the _____?
B. It's on/next to/near/over/under the _____.

[5, 28–32]
A. Where are the _____(s)?
B. They're on/next to/near/over/under the _____.

Do you like to work with tools?
What tools do you have in your home?

[1–16]
A. I can't find the **lawnmower**!
B. Look in the tool shed.
A. I did.
B. Oh! Wait a minute! I lent the **lawnmower** to the neighbors.

[17–32]
A. I can't find the **flashlight**!
B. Look in the utility cabinet.
A. I did.
B. Oh! Wait a minute! I lent the **flashlight** to the neighbors.

cortacésped/cortagrama/máquina cortadora de césped/de grama/de zacate	**1.**	lawnmower
lata de gasolina	**2.**	gas can
rociador/regadera	**3.**	sprinkler
manguera	**4.**	(garden) hose
pitón/pitongo/boca/boquilla	**5.**	nozzle
carretilla	**6.**	wheelbarrow
regadera	**7.**	watering can
rastrillo	**8.**	rake
azadón/azada	**9.**	hoe
palita de mano/palustre/palita de jardín	**10.**	trowel
pala	**11.**	shovel
tijeras de jardín	**12.**	hedge clippers
guantes de jardín	**13.**	work gloves
semillas	**14.**	vegetable seeds
abono	**15.**	fertilizer
semillas de césped/de grama/de zacate	**16.**	grass seed

linterna/lámpara/faro de mano	**17.**	flashlight
matamoscas	**18.**	fly swatter
extensión	**19.**	extension cord
cinta de medir	**20.**	tape measure
escalera	**21.**	step ladder
bomba desatapacaños/destascador/ destapacaños	**22.**	plunger
metro/vara de una yarda	**23.**	yardstick
trampa paracazar ratas/ratones/ratonera	**24.**	mousetrap
baterías	**25.**	batteries
foco/bombilla eléctrica	**26.**	lightbulbs/bulbs
fusibles	**27.**	fuses
cinta aisladora/de aislar/de empalme	**28.**	electrical tape
lubricante/aceite tres en uno	**29.**	oil
goma de pegar/pegamento	**30.**	glue
insecticida/aerosol para matar insectos	**31.**	bug spray/insect spray
matacucarachas/ aerosol para matarcucarachas	**32.**	roach killer

[1–11, 17–24]
A. I'm going to the hardware store. Can you think of anything we need?
B. Yes. We need a/an _____.
A. Oh, that's right.

[12–16, 25–32]
A. I'm going to the hardware store. Can you think of anything we need?
B. Yes. We need _____.
A. Oh, that's right.

What gardening tools and home supplies do you have? Tell about how and when you use each one.

NÚMEROS CARDINALES Y ORDINALES

Números Cardinales / **Cardinal Numbers**

1	one	11	eleven	21	twenty-one	101	one hundred (and) one
2	two	12	twelve	22	twenty-two	102	one hundred (and) two
3	three	13	thirteen	30	thirty	1,000	one thousand
4	four	14	fourteen	40	forty	10,000	ten thousand
5	five	15	fifteen	50	fifty	100,000	one hundred thousand
6	six	16	sixteen	60	sixty	1,000,000	one million
7	seven	17	seventeen	70	seventy		
8	eight	18	eighteen	80	eighty		
9	nine	19	nineteen	90	ninety		
10	ten	20	twenty	100	one hundred		

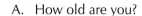

A. How old are you?

B. I'm _____ years old.

A. How many people are there in your family?

B. _____.

Números Ordinales / **Ordinal Numbers**

1st	first	11th	eleventh	21st	twenty-first	101st	one hundred (and) first
2nd	second	12th	twelfth	22nd	twenty-second	102nd	one hundred (and) second
3rd	third	13th	thirteenth	30th	thirtieth	1000th	one thousandth
4th	fourth	14th	fourteenth	40th	fortieth	10,000th	ten thousandth
5th	fifth	15th	fifteenth	50th	fiftieth	100,000th	one hundred thousandth
6th	sixth	16th	sixteenth	60th	sixtieth	1,000,000th	one millionth
7th	seventh	17th	seventeenth	70th	seventieth		
8th	eighth	18th	eighteenth	80th	eightieth		
9th	ninth	19th	nineteenth	90th	ninetieth		
10th	tenth	20th	twentieth	100th	one hundredth		

A. What floor do you live on?

B. I live on the _____ floor.

A. Is this the first time you've seen this movie?

B. No. It's the _____ time.

LAS MATEMÁTICAS

Aritmética / **Arithmetic**

suma addition	resta subtraction	multiplicación multiplication	división division
2 **plus** 1 **equals*** 3.	8 **minus** 3 **equals*** 5.	4 **times** 2 **equals*** 8.	10 **divided by** 2 **equals*** 5.

*You can also say: **is**

A. How much is *two plus one*?
B. *Two plus one* equals/is *three*.

Make conversations for the arithmetic problems above and others.

Fracciones / **Fractions**

one quarter/ one fourth	one third	one half/ half	two thirds	three quarters/ three fourths

A. Is this on sale?
B. Yes. It's _____ off the regular price.

A. Is the gas tank almost empty?
B. It's about _____ full.

Porcentajes / **Percents**

 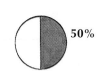  

twenty-five percent	fifty percent	seventy-five percent	one hundred percent

A. How did you do on the test?
B. I got _____ percent of the answers right.

A. What's the weather forecast?
B. There's a _____ percent chance of rain.

Research and discuss:
What percentage of the people in your country live in cities?
live on farms? work in factories? vote in national elections?

LA HORA

 2:00

two o'clock

 2:15

two fifteen/
a quarter after *two*

 2:30

two thirty/
half past *two*

 2:45

two forty-five
a quarter to *three*

 2:05

two oh five

 2:20

two twenty/
twenty after *two*

 2:40

two forty/
twenty to *three*

 2:55

two fifty-five
five to *three*

A. What time is it?
B. It's _____.

A. What time does the movie begin?
B. At _____.

two a.m.

two p.m.

noon/
twelve noon

midnight/
twelve midnight

A. When does the train leave?
B. At _____.

A. What time will we arrive?
B. At _____.

Tell about your daily schedule:
   What do you do? When?
   (I get up at _____. I ....)
Do you usually have enough time to do things, or do you run
   out of time? Explain.
If there were 25 hours in a day, what would you do with the
   extra hour? Why?

Tell about the use of time in different cultures or countries
you are familiar with:
   Do people arrive on time for work? appointments? parties?
   Do trains and buses operate exactly on schedule?
   Do movies and sports events begin on time?
   Do workplaces use time clocks or timesheets to record
   employees' work hours?

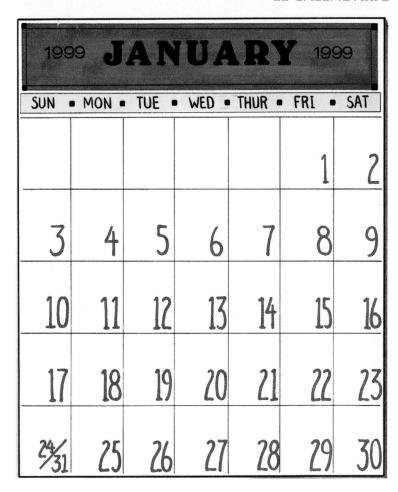

JANUARY 1999

SUN •	MON •	TUE •	WED •	THUR •	FRI •	SAT
					1	2
3	4	5	6	7	8	9
10	11	12	13	14	15	16
17	18	19	20	21	22	23
24/31	25	26	27	28	29	30

año 1. year

mil novecientos noventa y nueve — nineteen ninety-nine

mes 2. month

enero	January
febrero	February
marzo	March
abril	April
mayo	May
junio	June
julio	July
agosto	August
septiembre	September
octubre	October
noviembre	November
diciembre	December

días 3. day

domingo	Sunday
lunes	Monday
martes	Tuesday
miércoles	Wednesday
jueves	Thursday
viernes	Friday
sábado	Saturday

fecha 4. date

2 de enero de 1999	January 2, 1999
2/1/99	1/2/99
dos de enero de mil novecientos noventa y nueve	January second, nineteen ninety-nine

A. What year is it?
B. It's _____.

A. What month is it?
B. It's _____.

A. What day is it?
B. It's _____.

A. What's today's date?
B. Today is _____.

When did you begin to study English?
What days of the week do you study English? (I study English on _____.)

When is your birthday? (My birthday is on _____.)
What are your favorite months of the year? Why?
What are your least favorite months of the year? Why?

A. Where are you going?
B. I'm going to the **appliance store**.

tienda de electrodomésticos/ de artefactos/de enseres eléctricos	**1.** appliance store	cafetería	**8.** cafeteria
		guardería infantil	**9.** child-care center/day-care center
vendedor de autos	**2.** auto dealer/car dealer	tintorería/lavandería en seco	**10.** cleaners/dry cleaners
panadería/pastelería/repostería	**3.** bakery	tienda de donuts/donas	**11.** donut shop
banco	**4.** bank	clínica	**12.** clinic
barbería	**5.** barber shop	almacén	**13.** clothing store
librería	**6.** book store	cafetería	**14.** coffee shop
estación/terminal de autobuses	**7.** bus station	tienda de computadoras/ ordenadores	**15.** computer store

teatro	**16.** concert hall	gasolinera/surtidor/	**25.** gas station/
tienda/tiendita/taquería	**17.** convenience store	estación de gasolina	service station
centro/servicio de copiado/fotocopias	**18.** copy center	tienda/abarrotería/bodega/colmado	**26.** grocery store
salchichonería/tienda de embutidos	**19.** delicatessen/deli	salón de belleza/peluquería	**27.** hair salon
almacén	**20.** department store	ferretería	**28.** hardware store
tienda de descuentos	**21.** discount store	gimnasio/club	**29.** health club/spa
farmacia	**22.** drug store/pharmacy	hospital	**30.** hospital
floristería	**23.** flower shop/florist		
mueblería	**24.** furniture store		

A. Hi! How are you today?
B. Fine. Where are you going?
A. To the _____. How about you?
B. I'm going to the _____.

A. Oh, no! I can't find my wallet/purse!
B. Did you leave it at the _____?
A. Maybe I did.

Which of these places are in your neighborhood?
(In my neighborhood there's a/an ....)

A. Where's the **hotel**?
B. It's right over there.

 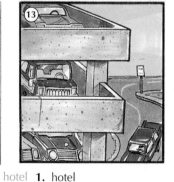  

hotel	**1.** hotel	cine	**8.** movie theater
heladería/refresquería/sorbetería	**2.** ice cream shop	museo	**9.** museum
joyería	**3.** jewelry store	almacén/tienda de música	**10.** music store
lavamático/lavandería pública	**4.** laundromat	club nocturno	**11.** night club
biblioteca	**5.** library	parque	**12.** park
almacén/tienda de ropa de	**6.** maternity shop	estacionamiento/garaje	**13.** (parking) garage
maternidad		estacionamiento	**14.** parking lot
motel	**7.** motel	tienda de animales domésticos/de mascotas	**15.** pet shop

fotocentro	**16.**	photo shop
pizzería	**17.**	pizza shop
edificio/oficina de correos/ el correo	**18.**	post office
restaurante	**19.**	restaurant
escuela	**20.**	school
zapatería/tienda de zapatos	**21.**	shoe store
centro comercial	**22.**	(shopping) mall
supermercado	**23.**	supermarket
teatro	**24.**	theater
juguetería	**25.**	toy store
estación del tren	**26.**	train station
agencia de viajes	**27.**	travel agency
videocentro	**28.**	video store
óptica	**29.**	vision center/eyeglass store
zoológico	**30.**	zoo

A. Is there a/an _____ nearby?
B. Yes. There's a/an _____ around the corner.

A. Excuse me. Where's the _____?
B. It's down the street, next to the _____.
A. Thank you.

Which of these places are in your neighborhood?
(In my neighborhood there's a/an ....)

A. Where's the _____?
B. On/In/Next to/Between/Across from/
   In front of/Behind/Under/Over the _____.

basurero	**1.** trash container	boca de la alcantarilla/alcantarilla/pozo	**11.** manhole	
estación de policía	**2.** police station	parada/paradero de autobuses/de guagoas	**12.** bus stop	
cárcel	**3.** jail	taxi	**13.** taxi/cab/taxicab	
juzgado/corte/tribunal	**4.** courthouse	taxista/conductor/chofer de taxi	**14.** taxi driver/cab driver	
banca/banco	**5.** bench	autobús/bus/guagua/camión	**15.** bus	
farol	**6.** street light	busero/conductor/chofer de autobús	**16.** bus driver	
repartidor de helados/carretilla de helados	**7.** ice cream truck	parquimetro/estaciónómetro	**17.** parking meter	
acera	**8.** sidewalk	inspectora de estaciónómetro	**18.** meter maid	
cuneta/cubeta	**9.** curb	subterráneo/metro	**19.** subway	
calle	**10.** street	estación del metro	**20.** subway station	

poste	**21.**	utility pole	cruce	**31.** intersection
parada de taxis/piquera	**22.**	taxi stand	policía	**32.** police officer
cabina de teléfonos	**23.**	phone booth	vía/paso peatonal/cruce de peatones/	**33.** crosswalk
teléfono público	**24.**	public telephone	línea de seguridad	
alcantarilla/desagüe/drenaje	**25.**	sewer	peatón	**34.** pedestrian
letrero con el nombre de la calle	**26.**	street sign	semáforo	**35.** traffic light/traffic signal
estación de bomberos	**27.**	fire station	camión de la basura	**36.** garbage truck
edificio de oficinas	**28.**	office building	puesto de periódicos	**37.** newsstand
cajero rápido/ventanilla de servicio rápido	**29.**	drive-through window	buhonero/vendedor ambulante	**38.** street vendor
alarma de incendios	**30.**	fire alarm box		

[An Election Speech]

If I am elected mayor, I'll take care of all the problems we have in our city. We need to do something about our _____s. We also need to do something about our _____s. And look at our _____s! We REALLY need to do something about THEM! We need a new mayor who can solve these problems. If I am elected mayor, we'll be proud of our _____s, _____s, and _____s again! Vote for me!

Step outside. Look around. Describe everything you see.

alto(a) – bajo(a) **1–2**	tall – short
largo(a) – corto(a) **3–4**	long – short
grande – chiquito(a)/pequeño(a) **5–6**	large/big – small/little
alto(a) – bajo(a) **7–8**	high – low
gordo(a) – flaco(a) **9–10**	heavy/fat – thin/skinny
pesado(a) – liviano(a) **11–12**	heavy – light
flojo(a) – estrecho(a)/apretado(a) **13–14**	loose – tight
rápido(a) – lento(a) **15–16**	fast – slow
recto(a) – curvo(a) **17–18**	straight – crooked
liso(a) – rizado(a) **19–20**	straight – curly
ancho(a) – angosto(a)/estrecho(a) **21–22**	wide – narrow
grueso(a) – delgado(a) **23–24**	thick – thin
oscuro(a) – claro(a)/con luz **25–26**	dark – light
nuevo(a) – viejo(a) **27–28**	new – old

joven – viejo(a) **29–30**	young – old
bueno(a)(s) – malo(a)(s) **31–32**	good – bad
caliente – frío(a) **33–34**	hot – cold
suave – duro(a) **35–36**	soft – hard
fácil – difícil **37–38**	easy – difficult/hard
liso(a) – áspero(a) **39–40**	smooth – rough
ordenado(a) – desordenado(a) **41–42**	neat – messy
limpio(a) – sucio(a) **43–44**	clean – dirty
escandaloso(a) – **45–46**	noisy/loud – quiet
quieto(a)/tranquilo(a)/callado(a)	
casado(a) – soltero(a) **47–48**	married – single
rico/adinerado – pobre **49–50**	rich/wealthy – poor

   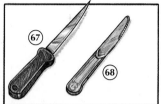

bonito(a) – feo(a)	**51–52**	pretty/beautiful – ugly
guapo(a) – feo(a)	**53–54**	handsome – ugly
mojado(a) – seco(a)	**55–56**	wet – dry
cerrado(a) – abierto(a)	**57–58**	open – closed
lleno(a) – vacío(a)	**59–60**	full – empty
caro(a) – barato(a)	**61–62**	expensive – cheap/inexpensive

elegante/adornado(a)/	**63–64**	fancy – plain
apuesto(a) – sencillo(a)		
brillante – opaco(a)	**65–66**	shiny – dull
afilado(a) – romo(a)	**67–68**	sharp – dull

[1–2]
A. Is your sister **tall**?
B. No. She's **short**.

1–2	Is your sister _____?
3–4	Is his hair _____?
5–6	Is their dog _____?
7–8	Is the bridge _____?
9–10	Is your friend _____?
11–12	Is the box _____?
13–14	Are the pants _____?
15–16	Is the train _____?
17–18	Is the path _____?
19–20	Is his hair _____?
21–22	Is that street _____?
23–24	Is the line _____?
25–26	Is the room _____?
27–28	Is your car _____?
29–30	Is he _____?
31–32	Are your neighbor's children _____?
33–34	Is the water _____?

35–36	Is your pillow _____?
37–38	Is today's homework _____?
39–40	Is your skin _____?
41–42	Is your desk _____?
43–44	Are the dishes _____?
45–46	Is your neighbor _____?
47–48	Is your sister _____?
49–50	Is your uncle _____?
51–52	Is the witch _____?
53–54	Is the pirate _____?
55–56	Are the clothes _____?
57–58	Is the door _____?
59–60	Is the pitcher _____?
61–62	Is that restaurant _____?
63–64	Is the dress _____?
65–66	Is your kitchen floor _____?
67–68	Is the knife _____?

A. Tell me about your ....
B. He's/She's/It's/They're _____.

A. Is your .... _____?
B. No, not at all. As a matter of
fact, he's/she's/it's/they're
_____.

Describe yourself.
Describe a person you know.
Describe one of your favorite places.

A. You look **tired**.
B. I am. I'm VERY **tired**.

cansado(a)	**1.** tired		enfermo(a)	**9.** sick/ill
soñoliento (a)	**2.** sleepy		contento(a)	**10.** happy
agotado(a)	**3.** exhausted		feliz	**11.** ecstatic
tener calor	**4.** hot		triste	**12.** sad/unhappy
tener frío	**5.** cold		hastiado(a)	**13.** miserable
tener hambre	**6.** hungry		satisfecho(a)	**14.** pleased
tener sed/sediento	**7.** thirsty		decepcionado(a)	**15.** disappointed
estar lleno	**8.** full		contrariado(a)	**16.** upset

molesto(a)/contrariado(a)	**17.** annoyed	preocupado(a)	**25.** worried
frustrado(a)	**18.** frustrated	asustado(a)/con miedo	**26.** scared/afraid
furioso(a)/enfadado(a)/disgustado(a)	**19.** angry/mad	aburrido(a)	**27.** bored
furioso(a)	**20.** furious	orgulloso(a)	**28.** proud
harto(a)/colmado(a)/asqueado	**21.** disgusted	avergonzado(a)	**29.** embarrassed
sorprendido(a)	**22.** surprised	apenado(a)	**30.** ashamed
atónito(a)/turbado(a)/consternado(a)/ estupefacto/pasmado	**23.** shocked	celoso(a)	**31.** jealous
nervioso(a)	**24.** nervous	enredado(a)/confundido(a)	**32.** confused

A. Are you _____?
B. No. Why do you ask? Do I LOOK _____?
A. Yes. You do.

A. I'm _____.
B. Why?
A. ....

What makes you happy? sad? mad?
When do you feel nervous? annoyed?
Do you ever feel embarrassed? When?

LAS FRUTAS

[1–22]

A. This **apple** is delicious!
   Where did you get it?

B. At *Shaw's Supermarket.*

[23–31]

A. These **grapes** are delicious!
   Where did you get them?

B. At *Farmer Fred's Fruit Stand.*

manzana	**1.** apple	coco	**12.** coconut	mandarina	**22.** tangerine
melocotón	**2.** peach	aguacate	**13.** avocado	uvas	**23.** grapes
pera	**3.** pear	melón	**14.** cantaloupe	cerezas	**24.** cherries
banana/guineo/plátano	**4.** banana	melón verde/dulce	**15.** honeydew (melon)	ciruelas pasas	**25.** prunes
ciruela	**5.** plum	piña	**16.** pineapple	dátiles	**26.** dates
albaricoque	**6.** apricot	sandía/melón de agua	**17.** watermelon	uvas pasas/pasitas	**27.** raisins
nectarina	**7.** nectarine	toronja	**18.** grapefruit	arándano	**28.** blueberries
kiwi	**8.** kiwi	limón (amarillo)	**19.** lemon	arándano agrio	**29.** cranberries
papaya/fruta bomba	**9.** papaya	lima/limón verde	**20.** lime	frambuesas	**30.** raspberries
mango	**10.** mango	naranja/china	**21.** orange	fresas	**31.** strawberries
higo	**11.** fig				

A. I'm hungry. Do we have any fruit?
B. Yes. We have _____s* and _____s.*

*With 14–18, use:
  We have _____ and _____.

A. Do we have any more _____s?†
B. No. I'll get some more when I go to the supermarket.

†With 14–18, use:
  Do we have any more _____?

What are your most favorite fruits?
What are your least favorite fruits?
Which of these fruits grow where you live?
Name and describe other fruits you are familiar with.

LOS VEGETALES

A. What do we need from the supermarket?
B. We need **lettuce*** and **peas**.†

*1–12   †13–36

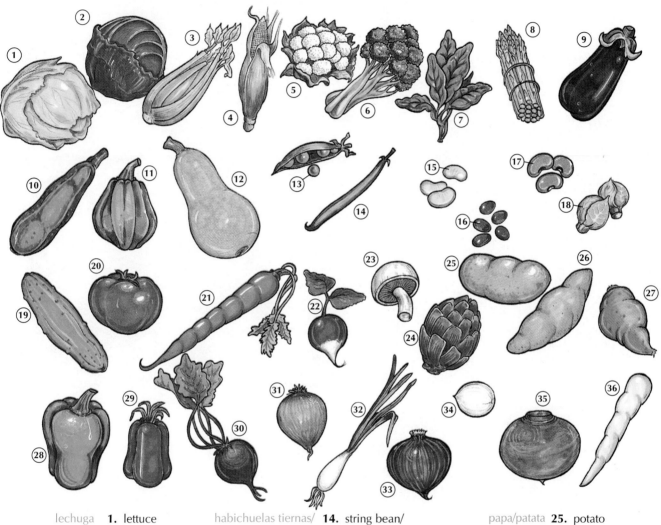

lechuga	**1.** lettuce	habichuelas tiernas/	**14.** string bean/	papa/patata **25.** potato
repollo/col	**2.** cabbage	ejotes/judías verdes	green bean	boniato/camote/batata **26.** sweet potato
apio	**3.** celery	haba	**15.** lima bean	papa dulce/batata **27.** yam
maíz/elote	**4.** corn	frijol negro	**16.** black bean	pimiento verde **28.** green pepper
coliflor	**5.** cauliflower	frijol rojo/colorado/	**17.** kidney bean	pimiento rojo/ **29.** red pepper
brócoli/brécol	**6.** broccoli	habichuelas coloradas/		pimiento morron
espinaca	**7.** spinach	poroto		remolacha **30.** beet
espárrago	**8.** asparagus	repollito/col de bruselas	**18.** brussels sprout	cebolla **31.** onion
berenjena	**9.** eggplant	pepino/pepinillo	**19.** cucumber	cebollino(a)/cebollin/ **32.** scallion/green onion
calabacita/calabacín	**10.** zucchini (squash)	tomate	**20.** tomato	escalonia
calabaza pequeña	**11.** acorn squash	zanahoria	**21.** carrot	cebolla morada **33.** red onion
zapallo	**12.** butternut squash	rábano	**22.** radish	cebollita/cebolla blanca **34.** pearl onion
guisante/chícharo/	**13.** pea	hongo/seta	**23.** mushroom	nabo **35.** turnip
petit pois		alcachofa	**24.** artichoke	nabo/pastinaca **36.** parsnip

A. How do you like the
   [1–12] / [13–36] s?
B. It's/They're delicious.

A. *Johnny?* Finish your vegetables!
B. But you KNOW I hate
   [1–12] / [13–36] s!
A. I know. But it's/they're good
   for you!

Which vegetables do you like?
Which vegetables don't you like?
Which of these vegetables grow where
   you live?
Name and describe other vegetables
   you are familiar with.

A. I'm going to the supermarket to get **milk** and **soup**.*
   Do we need anything else?

B. Yes. We also need **cereal** and **soda**.*

*With 43, 44, 46, 49, and 55, use: a _____.

Productos lácteos	**A. Dairy Products**	Productos enlatados	**B. Canned Goods**	Jugos	**D. Juice**
leche	**1.** milk	sopa	**15.** soup	jugo de manzana	**26.** apple juice
leche baja en grasas	**2.** low-fat milk	tuna enlatada/atún	**16.** tuna fish	jugo de piña	**27.** pineapple juice
leche descremada/	**3.** skim milk	enlatado		jugo de toronja	**28.** grapefruit juice
leche desgrasada/		vegetales enlatados	**17.** (canned) vegetables	jugo de tomate	**29.** tomato juice
leche sin grasa		fruta enlatada	**18.** (canned) fruit	ponche de frutas	**30.** fruit punch
leche con chocolate	**4.** chocolate milk			jugo de uvas	**31.** grape juice
leche agria/	**5.** buttermilk	Productos evasados	**C. Packaged Goods**	jugo de arándano	**32.** cranberry juice
leche con suero		cereal	**19.** cereal	agrio	
jugo de naranja/	**6.** orange juice	galletas	**20.** cookies	cartón de seis jugos/	**33.** juice paks
de china		galletas de soda	**21.** crackers	paquete de seis jugos	
queso	**7.** cheese	pasta/espaguetis	**22.** spaghetti	jugo en polvo	**34.** powdered
mantequilla	**8.** butter	fideos/tallarines	**23.** noodles		drink mix
margarina	**9.** margarine	macarrones cortos/	**24.** macaroni		
crema agria	**10.** sour cream	coditos		Bebidas	**E. Beverages**
queso crema	**11.** cream cheese	arroz	**25.** rice	soda/gaseosa	**35.** soda
requesón	**12.** cottage cheese			soda de dieta	**36.** diet soda
yogur/leche búlgara	**13.** yogurt			agua embotellada	**37.** bottled water
huevos	**14.** eggs				

† Orange juice is not a dairy product, but is usually found in this section.

Aves	**F. Poultry**		puerco/cerdo	**51.** pork		mejillones	**66.** mussels
gallina/pollo	**38.** chicken		chuletas de puerco/de cerdo	**52.** pork chops		almejas	**67.** clams
encuentro y muslo	**39.** chicken legs		costillas	**53.** ribs		cangrejos	**68.** crabs
de gallina/muslo y			salchichones/chorizos/	**54.** sausages		langosta	**69.** lobster
cadera de pollo			longaniza/salchichas				
muslos de gallina/	**40.** drumsticks		jamón	**55.** ham		**Panadería y pastelería**	**I. Baked Goods**
de pollo			tocino/tocineta	**56.** bacon			
pechugas de gallina/	**41.** chicken breasts					panecillo inglés	**70.** English muffins
de pollo			**Pescados y mariscos**	**H. Seafood**		torta/bizcocho	**71.** cake
alitas/alas de gallina/	**42.** chicken wings		PESCADOS	FISH		pan de pita	**72.** pita bread
de pollo			salmón	**57.** salmon		panecillos	**73.** rolls
pavo	**43.** turkey		mero	**58.** halibut		pan	**74.** bread
pato	**44.** duck		lenguado	**59.** flounder			
			pez espada	**60.** swordfish		**Productos congelados**	**J. Frozen Foods**
Carnes	**G. Meat**		abadejo	**61.** haddock		helado	**75.** ice cream
carne molida	**45.** ground beef		trucha	**62.** trout		vegetales congelados	**76.** frozen vegetables
carne para asar	**46.** roast					comida congelada/platos	**77.** frozen dinners
filete/biftec/bistec/	**47.** steak		MARISCOS	SHELLFISH		congelados	
bisté/bife			ostras	**63.** oysters		(concentrado de)	**78.** frozen lemonade
carne para guisar	**48.** stewing meat		conchuelas/	**64.** scallops		limonada congelada	
pierna de cordero	**49.** leg of lamb		vieiras/veneras			(concentrado de) jugo	**79.** frozen orange
chuletas de cordero	**50.** lamb chops		camarones/langostinos	**65.** shrimp		de naranja/china congelado	juice

A. Excuse me. Where can I find
   [1–79] ?
B. In the [A–J] Section, next to
   the [1–79] .
A. Thank you.

A. Pardon me. I'm looking for
   [1–79] .
B. It's/They're in the [A–J]
   Section, between the
   [1–79] and the [1–79] .
A. Thanks.

Which of these foods do you like?
Which foods are good for you?
What brands of these foods do you
   buy?

[1–70]

A. Look! _____ is/are on sale this week!

B. Let's get some!

Quesos, embutidos y platos preparados	**A. Deli**		**Refrigerios/botanas/antojitos/ comida para picar/saladitos**		**B. Snack Foods**
asado de carne/rosbif	**1.**	roast beef	papas fritas/papitas	**16.**	potato chips
mortadela	**2.**	bologna	fritos de maíz	**17.**	corn chips
salami	**3.**	salami	fritos de tortilla	**18.**	tortilla chips
jamón	**4.**	ham	fritos de nacho	**19.**	nacho chips
pavo	**5.**	turkey	galletas tostadas	**20.**	pretzels
carne adobada/ en salmuera/ salpresa/cornbif	**6.**	corned beef	cubiertas con sal/ pretzels		
queso americano	**7.**	American cheese	rosetas/palomitas/hojuelas/ rositas de maíz/millo	**21.**	popcorn
queso suizo	**8.**	Swiss cheese	nueces	**22.**	nuts
provolone	**9.**	provolone	maní/cacahuetes	**23.**	peanuts
mozzarela	**10.**	mozzarella			
queso Cheddar	**11.**	cheddar cheese	**Condimentos/especies**		**C. Condiments**
ensalada de papas/ de patatas	**12.**	potato salad	salsa de tomate	**24.**	ketchup
ensalada de repollo	**13.**	cole slaw	mostaza	**25.**	mustard
ensalada de pasta/ de coditos	**14.**	macaroni salad	encurtido picado	**26.**	relish
			encurtidos	**27.**	pickles
ensalada de mariscos	**15.**	seafood salad	aceitunas	**28.**	olives
			sal	**29.**	salt
			pimienta	**30.**	pepper
			condimentos/especies	**31.**	spices
			salsa china/de soya	**32.**	soy sauce

mayonesa	**33.**	mayonnaise
aceite para cocinar	**34.**	(cooking) oil
aceite de oliva	**35.**	olive oil
vinagre	**36.**	vinegar
aliño/aderezo para ensaladas	**37.**	salad dressing

Café y té	**D. Coffee and Tea**	
café	**38.**	coffee
café descafeinado	**39.**	decaffeinated coffee/decaf coffee
té	**40.**	tea
tisana/infusión de hierbas/ de yerbas	**41.**	herbal tea
chocolate caliente	**42.**	cocoa/hot chocolate mix

Productos para hornear	**E. Baking Products**	
harina	**43.**	flour
azúcar	**44.**	sugar
mezcla para tortas o bizcochos en paquete	**45.**	cake mix

Mermeladas y jaleas	**F. Jams and Jellies**	papel de plástico	**62.** plastic wrap	cupones	**76.** coupons
mermelada	**46.** jam	papel encerado/de cera	**63.** waxed paper	etiquetador/detector de precios electrónico	**77.** scanner
jalea	**47.** jelly				
mermelada (con trozos de fruta)	**48.** marmalade	**Artículos para niños**	**I. Baby Products**	pesa/balanza	**78.** scale
mantequilla de maní/ de cacahuete	**49.** peanut butter	cereal	**64.** baby cereal	caja/registradora	**79.** cash register
		fórmula	**65.** formula	cajera	**80.** cashier
		papillas/comidas de bebé en frasquitos o tarritos/colados	**66.** baby food	bolsa plástica	**81.** plastic bag
Artículos de papel	**G. Paper Products**			bolsa/cartucho de papel/talego	**82.** paper bag
pañuelos de papel/ Kleenex	**50.** tissues	servilletas/ toallitas desechables	**67.** wipes	empacador	**83.** bagger/packer
servilletas	**51.** napkins	pañales desechables	**68.** (disposable) diapers	fila rápida/ expreso	**84.** express checkout (line)
papel higiénico	**52.** toilet paper	**Comida para mascotas**	**J. Pet Food**	periódico	**85.** tabloid (newspaper)
vasos de papel	**53.** paper cups	comida para gatos	**69.** cat food		
platos de cartón	**54.** paper plates	comida para perros	**70.** dog food	revista	**86.** magazine
pajilla/popote/carrizo/ absorbente	**55.** straws	**Área de salida**	**K. Checkout Area**	chicle/goma de masticar/mascar/ chingongo	**87.** (chewing) gum
papel toalla	**56.** paper towels	corredor/sección	**71.** aisle		
		carretilla/carrito	**72.** shopping cart	pastilla/ caramelo/dulce	**88.** candy
Auxiliares domésticos	**H. Household Items**	cliente	**73.** shopper/customer		
bolsas/bolsitas plásticas	**57.** sandwich bags	caja/mostrador de chequeo/de caja	**74.** checkout counter	canasto(a)/cesto(a)/ bolsa/talego/ cartucho	**89.** shopping basket
bolsas para la basura	**58.** trash bags	banda/cinta transportadora	**75.** conveyor belt		
jabón	**59.** soap				
jabón líquido	**60.** liquid soap				
papel de aluminio	**61.** aluminum foil				

A. Do we need __[1–70]__ ?
B. No, but we need __[1–70]__ .

A. We forgot to get __[1–70]__ !
B. I'll get it/them.
   Where is it?/Where are they?
A. In the __[A–J]__ Section over there.

Make a complete shopping list of everything you need from the supermarket.
Describe the differences between U.S. supermarkets and food stores in your country.

ENVASES Y MEDIDAS

A. Would you please get a **bag** of *flour* when you go to the supermarket?

B. A **bag** of *flour*? Sure. I'd be happy to.

A. Would you please get two **head**s of *lettuce* when you go to the supermarket?

B. Two **head**s of *lettuce*? Sure. I'd be happy to.

bolsa	**1.** bag	racimo/manojo/mazo **5.** bunch	docena **9.** dozen*
barra	**2.** bar	lata **6.** can	mazorca **10.** ear
botella	**3.** bottle	cartón **7.** carton	cabeza **11.** head
caja/cajeta/cajetita	**4.** box	envase **8.** container	frasco/tarro/pote **12.** jar

* "a dozen eggs," NOT "a dozen of eggs."

hogaza de pan	**13.** loaf–loaves	cartón/paquete/	**17.** six-pack	cuarto	**21.** quart
paquete/cajetilla/	**14.** pack	bulto de seis artículos		medio galón	**22.** half-gallon
cajeta		barra	**18.** stick	galón	**23.** gallon
paquete/bulto	**15.** package	bote	**19.** tub	litro	**24.** liter
rollo	**16.** roll	pinta	**20.** pint	libra	**25.** pound

[At home]	[In a supermarket]	Open your kitchen cabinets and
A. What did you get at the	A. Is this checkout counter open?	refrigerator. Make a list of all the
supermarket?	B. Yes, but this is the express line.	things you find.
B. I got _____, _____, and	Do you have more than eight items?	What do you do with empty bottles,
_____.	B. No. I only have _____,	jars, and cans? Do you recycle them,
	_____, and _____.	reuse them, or throw them away?

PESOS Y MEDIDAS

cucharadita
cdta.
teaspoon
tsp.

cucharada
cda.
tablespoon
Tbsp.

una onza
1 oz. líquida
1 (fluid) ounce
1 fl. oz.

una taza
8 ozs. líquidas
cup
8 fl. ozs.

una pinta
16 ozs. líquidas
pint
pt.
16 fl. ozs.

una pinta
32 ozs. líquidas
quart
qt.
32 fl. ozs.

un galón
128 ozs. líquidas
gallon
gal.
128 fl. ozs.

A.   How much water should I put in?
B.   The recipe says to add one _____ of water.

A.   This fruit punch is delicious! What's in it?
B.   Two _____s of orange juice, three _____s of grape juice, and a _____ of apple juice.

una onza
1 oz.

un cuarto de libra
1/4 lb.
4 ozs.

media libra
1/2 lb.
8 ozs.

tres cuartos de libra
3/4 lb.
12 ozs.

una libra
1 lb.
16 ozs.

an ounce
oz.

a quarter
of a pound
¼ lb.
4 ozs.

half a pound
½ lb.
8 ozs.

three-quarters
of a pound
¾ lb.
12 ozs.

a pound
lb.
16 ozs.

A.   How much roast beef would you like?
B.   I'd like _____, please.

A.   This chili tastes very good! What did you put in it?
B.   _____ of ground beef, _____ of beans, _____ of tomatoes, and _____ of chili powder.

A. Can I help?
B. Yes. Please **cut up** the *vegetables.*

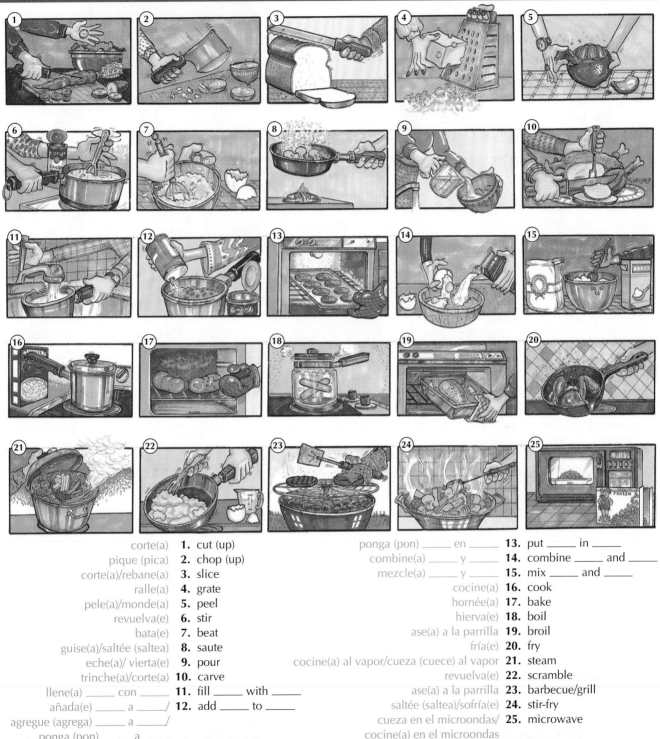

corte(a)	**1.** cut (up)	ponga (pon) _____ en _____	**13.** put _____ in _____
pique (pica)	**2.** chop (up)	combine(a) _____ y _____	**14.** combine _____ and _____
corte(a)/rebane(a)	**3.** slice	mezcle(a) _____ y _____	**15.** mix _____ and _____
ralle(a)	**4.** grate	cocine(a)	**16.** cook
pele(a)/monde(a)	**5.** peel	hornée(a)	**17.** bake
revuelva(e)	**6.** stir	hierva(e)	**18.** boil
bata(e)	**7.** beat	ase(a) a la parrilla	**19.** broil
guise(a)/saltée (saltea)	**8.** saute	fría(e)	**20.** fry
eche(a)/ vierta(e)	**9.** pour	cocine(a) al vapor/cueza (cuece) al vapor	**21.** steam
trinche(a)/corte(a)	**10.** carve	revuelva(e)	**22.** scramble
llene(a) _____ con _____	**11.** fill _____ with _____	ase(a) a la parrilla	**23.** barbecue/grill
añada(e) _____ a _____/	**12.** add _____ to _____	saltée (saltea)/sofría(e)	**24.** stir-fry
agregue (agrega) _____ a _____/		cueza en el microondas/	**25.** microwave
ponga (pon) _____ a_____		cocine(a) en el microondas	

[1–25] A. What are you doing?
　　　　B. I'm _____ing the ....

[16–25] A. How long should I _____ the ....?
　　　　　B. For .... minutes/seconds.

What's your favorite recipe? Give instructions and use the units of measure on page 52. For example:

Mix a cup of flour and two tablespoons of sugar.
Add half a pound of butter.
Bake at 350° (degrees) for twenty minutes.

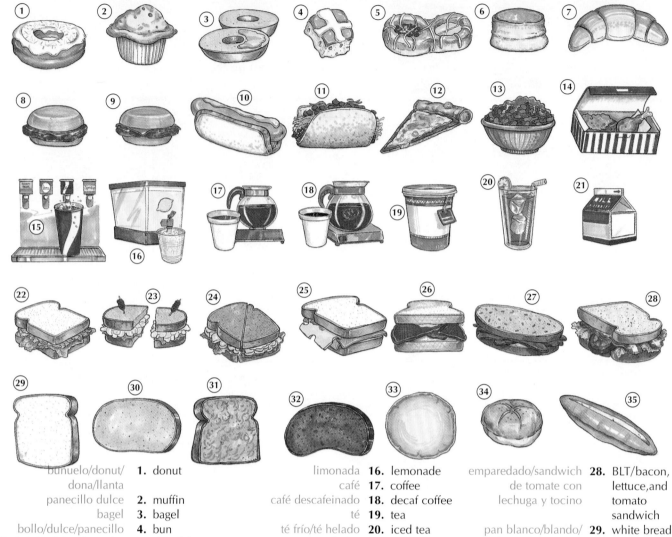

buñuelo/donut/	**1.** donut	limonada	**16.** lemonade	emparedado/sandwich	**28.** BLT/bacon,
dona/llanta		café	**17.** coffee	de tomate con	lettuce,and
panecillo dulce	**2.** muffin	café descafeinado	**18.** decaf coffee	lechuga y tocino	tomato
bagel	**3.** bagel	té	**19.** tea		sandwich
bollo/dulce/panecillo	**4.** bun	té frío/té helado	**20.** iced tea	pan blanco/blando/	**29.** white bread
variedad de dulces/pasteles	**5.** danish/pastry	leche	**21.** milk	suave/del mondo/de agua	
bisquet/panecillo	**6.** biscuit	emparedado/sandwich	**22.** tuna fish sandwich	pan de centeno	**30.** rye bread
croissant	**7.** croissant	de tuna o atún		pan integral	**31.** whole wheat
hamburguesa	**8.** hamburger	emparedado/sandwich	**23.** egg salad	de trigo	bread
quesoburguesa/	**9.** cheeseburger	de huevo	sandwich	pan integral de centeno/	**32.** pumpernickel
hamburguesa con queso		emparedado/sandwich	**24.** chicken salad	pan de centeno entero	
perro caliente/hot dog	**10.** hot dog	de pollo	sandwich	pan de pita/pan sirio	**33.** pita bread
taco	**11.** taco	emparedado/sandwich	**25.** ham and cheese	un panecito/	**34.** a roll
tajada/pedazo/	**12.** slice of pizza	de jamón con queso	sandwich	un panecillo/	
porción de pizza/		emparedado/sandwich	**26.** roast beef	un bollo/	
ración/plato/tazón de chile	**13.** bowl of chili	de carne (asada)	sandwich	un mollete/un panecito/	**35.** a submarine
orden de pollo frito	**14.** order of fried chicken	emparedado/	**27.** corned beef	un pan de barra	roll
soda/gaseosa/Coca Cola/	**15.** Coke/Diet Coke/	sandwich	sandwich		
Pepsi/Seven up	Pepsi/7–Up/…	de carne abobada en			
		salmuera (cornbif)			

A. May I help you?
B. Yes. I'd like a/an [1–14] , please.
A. Anything to drink?
B. Yes. I'll have a small/medium-size/
large/extra-large [15–21] .

A. I'd like a [22–28] on [29–35] , please.
B. What do you want on it?
A. Lettuce/tomato/mayonnaise/mustard/…

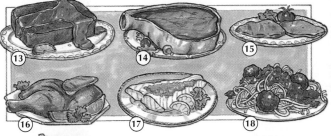

Entradas/Abrebocas/Aperitivos **Appetizers**

coctel/copa 1. fruit cup/ alitas de pollo 4. chicken wings
de frutas   fruit cocktail   nachos 5. nachos
jugo de tomate 2. tomato juice cáscaras de 6. potato skins
coctel de camarones/ 3. shrimp   papa rellenas
de gambas   cocktail

Ensaladas **Salads**

ensalada mixta 7. tossed salad/ antipasto 10. antipasto
    garden salad ensalada 11. Caesar salad
ensalada griega 8. Greek salad estilo César
ensalada de 9. spinach salad barra de 12. salad bar
espinacas   ensalada

Plato Fuerte **Main Courses/Entrees**

pastel/budín de 13. meatloaf pollo al horno/ 16. baked chicken
carne molida   pollo asado
filete/bistec de 14. roast beef/ pescado a la 17. broiled fish
costilla asado/rosbif   prime rib parrilla
chuleta de ternera 15. veal cutlet espaguetis 18. spaghetti

Acompañamientos **Side Dishes**

una papa 19. a baked arroz 22. rice
al horno/asada   potato fideos 23. noodles
puré de papas 20. mashed vegetales 24. mixed
papas majadas   potatoes mixtos   vegetab;es
papas fritas/ 21. french fries
papas estilo francés

Postres **Dessert**

bizcocho/torta/ 25. chocolate gelatina 28. jello
pastel de chocolate   cake pudín 29. pudding
pastel/tarta de 26. apple pie copa de 30. ice cream
manzanas   helado especial/   sundae
helado 27. ice cream sundae

[Ordering dinner]
A. May I take your order?
B. Yes, please. For the appetizer I'd like the [1–6] .
A. And what kind of salad would you like?
B. I'll have the [7–12] .
A. And for the main course?
B. I'd like the [13–18] , please.
A. What side dish would you like with that?
B. Hmm. I think I'll have [19–24] .

[Ordering dessert]
A. Would you care for some dessert?
B. Yes. I'll have [25–29] /an [30] .

Do you go to restaurants? Which ones? What do you order? Describe some popular desserts in your country.

COLORS
LOS COLORES

A. What's your favorite color?
B. **Red.**

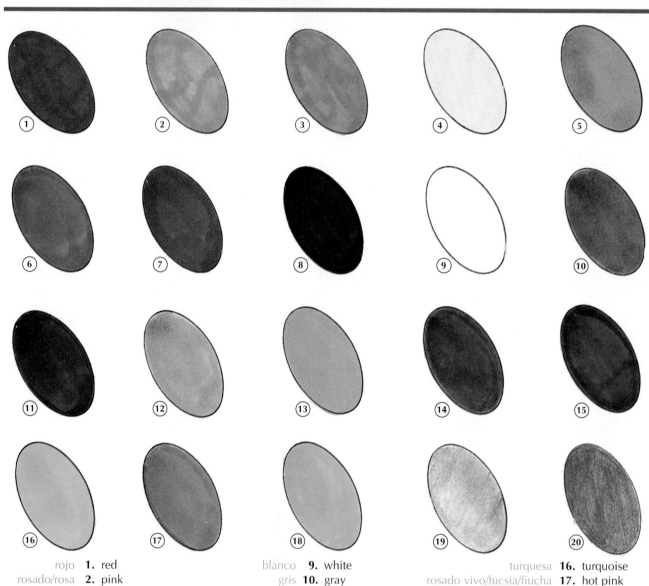

rojo **1.** red	blanco **9.** white	turquesa **16.** turquoise
rosado/rosa **2.** pink	gris **10.** gray	rosado vivo/fucsia/fiucha **17.** hot pink
anaranjado **3.** orange	marrón/chocolate/ **11.** brown	verde eléctrico/verde **18.** neon green
amarillo **4.** yellow	pardo/café/carmelita	fosforescente/verde neón
verde **5.** green	crema/beige **12.** beige	plateado **19.** silver
azul **6.** blue	verde claro **13.** light green	dorado **20.** gold
morado/violeta **7.** purple	verde oscuro **14.** dark green	
negro **8.** black	azul marino **15.** navy blue	

A. I like your _____ shirt.
You look very good in _____.
B. Thank you. _____ is my favorite color.

A. My color TV is broken.
B. What's the matter with it?
A. People's faces are _____, the sky is _____, and the grass is _____!

Do you know the flags of different countries? What are the colors of the flags you know?
What color makes you happy? What color makes you sad? Why?

LA ROPA

A. I think I'll wear my new **shirt** today.
B. Good idea!

camisa/camisa de mangas largas	**1.** shirt/long-sleeved shirt	suéter/jersey con **17.** V-neck sweater
camisa de mangas cortas	**2.** short-sleeved shirt	cuello de pico
camisa de vestir	**3.** dress shirt	suéter abierto **18.** cardigan sweater
camisa de sport/camisa hawaiana	**4.** sport shirt	overol/mono/mameluco **19.** overalls
polo/niqui/jersey de punto/suéter	**5.** polo shirt/jersey/sport shirt	uniforme **20.** uniform
camisa de franela/de lanilla	**6.** flannel shirt	saco/chaqueta/chaquetón/ **21.** jacket/sports jacket/
blusa	**7.** blouse	campera/americana sports coat
camisa de cuello de	**8.** turtleneck	saco/chaqueta **22.** jacket
tortuga/de cisne		saco/chaquetón sport/ **23.** blazer
pantalones	**9.** pants/slacks	con botones cruzados
pantalones de mezclila/	**10.** (blue) jeans	traje/vestido **24.** suit
pantalones de dril/		conjunto/traje/vestido de tres **25.** three-piece suit
jeans/mahones		piezas/terno
pantalones de pana/	**11.** corduroy pants/	chaleco **26.** vest
de cordeoneillo	corduroys	corbata **27.** tie/necktie
falda	**12.** skirt	corbatita de gato/ **28.** bowtie
traje/vestido	**13.** dress	corbatín/mariquita/corbata de
mono/mameluco	**14.** jumpsuit	pajarita/corbata de lazo
pantalones cortos	**15.** shorts	esmoquin/smoking **29.** tuxedo
jersey/suéter cerrado/	**16.** sweater	traje/vestido de noche/de fiesta/ **30.** (evening) gown
de cuello redondo		formal/de etiqueta

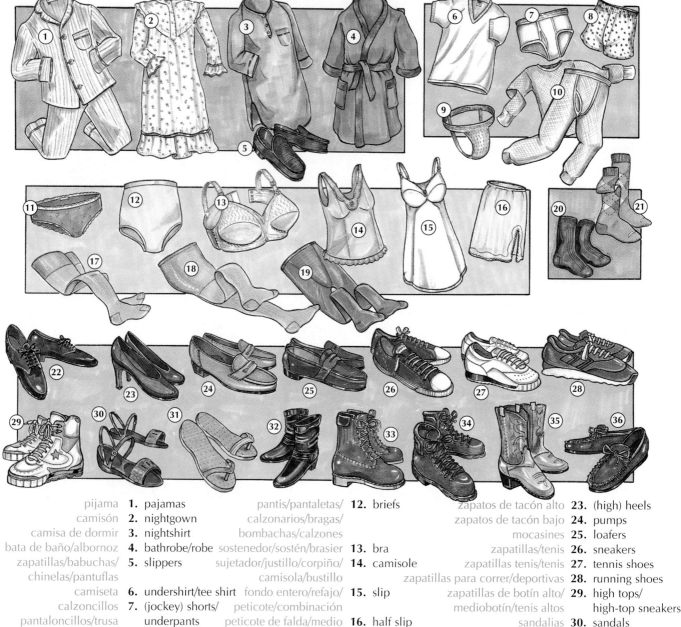

pijama	**1.** pajamas	pantis/pantaletas/	**12.** briefs	zapatos de tacón alto	**23.** (high) heels
camisón	**2.** nightgown	calzonarios/bragas/		zapatos de tacón bajo	**24.** pumps
camisa de dormir	**3.** nightshirt	bombachas/calzones		mocasines	**25.** loafers
bata de baño/albornoz	**4.** bathrobe/robe	sostenedor/sostén/brasier	**13.** bra	zapatillas/tenis	**26.** sneakers
zapatillas/babuchas/	**5.** slippers	sujetador/justillo/corpiño/	**14.** camisole	zapatillas tenis/tenis	**27.** tennis shoes
chinelas/pantuflas		camisola/bustillo		zapatillas para correr/deportivas	**28.** running shoes
camiseta	**6.** undershirt/tee shirt	fondo entero/refajo/	**15.** slip	zapatillas de botín alto/	**29.** high tops/
calzoncillos	**7.** (jockey) shorts/	peticote/combinación		mediobotín/tenis altos	high-top sneakers
pantaloncillos/trusa	underpants	peticote de falda/medio	**16.** half slip	sandalias	**30.** sandals
calzoncillos/pantaloncillos	**8.** boxer shorts	fondo/enagua		chancletas/chinelas/	**31.** thongs/flip-flops
boxer/largos		medias	**17.** stockings	pantunflas	
suspensorios	**9.** athletic supporter/	pantimedia	**18.** pantyhose	botas	**32.** boots
	jock strap	leotardos/mallas	**19.** tights	botas de trabajo	**33.** work boots
calzón	**10.** long underwear/	calcetines/medias	**20.** socks	botas para escalar	**34.** hiking boots
	long johns	calcetines largos/medias	**21.** knee socks	botas estilo vaquero/	**35.** cowboy boots
panti bikini/	**11.** (bikini) panties/	tobilleras/tobimedias		de vaquero	
pantaleta bikini	underpants	zapatos	**22.** shoes	mocasines	**36.** moccasins

[1–21] A. I can't find my new _____.
B. Did you look in the bureau/dresser/closet?
A. Yes, I did.
B. Then it's/they're probably in the wash.

[22–36] A. Are those new _____?
B. Yes, they are.
A. They're very nice.
B. Thanks.

ROPA PARA HACER EJERCICIOS, DEPORTES Y PARA RESGUARDARSE DEL TIEMPO

camiseta/playera	**1.** tee shirt	leotardo	**10.** tights	guantes	**25.** gloves
camiseta sin mangas	**2.** tank top	bandana/vincha	**11.** sweatband	mitones/	**26.** mittens
sudadera	**3.** sweatshirt	chaqueta/chamarra	**12.** coat	guantes enteros	
pantalones de sudadera	**4.** sweat pants	sobretodo/abrigo/gabán	**13.** overcoat	sombrero	**27.** hat
pantalones cortos/	**5.** running	chaqueta/campera/chompa	**14.** jacket	gorra/cachucha	**28.** cap
pantaloncillos/calzonas	shorts	rompeviento/chompa	**15.** windbreaker	gorra de béisbol	**29.** baseball cap
deportivas/shorts		chaqueta de esquiar	**16.** ski jacket	boina	**30.** beret
pantalones cortos/	**6.** tennis shorts	chaqueta de cuero	**17.** bomber jacket	sombrero	**31.** rain hat
pantaloncillos/		abrigo/chamarra de invierno	**18.** parka	impermeable	
shorts para jugar tenis		chaqueta	**19.** down jacket	gorro/	**32.** ski hat
pantalones cortos/	**7.** lycra shorts	chaleco de plumas de ganso	**20.** down vest	gorra de esquiar	
pantaloncillos/		capote/impermeable	**21.** raincoat	pasamontañas/	**33.** ski mask
shorts de lycra		poncho	**22.** poncho	máscara de esquiar	
traje para correr	**8.** jogging/running suit	gabardina/impermeable	**23.** trenchcoat	orejeras	**34.** ear muffs
leotardo	**9.** leotard	zapatos de goma/	**24.** rubbers	bufanda	**35.** scarf
		de caucho para la lluvia			

[1–11]

A. Excuse me. I found this/these _____
in the dryer. Is it/Are they yours?

B. Yes. It's/They're mine. Thank you.

[12–35]

A. What's the weather like today?

B. It's cool/cold/raining/snowing.

A. I think I'll wear my _____.

A. Oh, no! I think I lost my **ring**!
B. I'll help you look for it.

A. Oh, no! I think I lost my **earrings**!
B. I'll help you look for them.

anillo/sortija	**1.** ring
anillo/sortija de compromiso	**2.** engagement ring
anillo/sortija de matrimonio	**3.** wedding ring/wedding band
aretes/pendientes/pantallas	**4.** earrings
collar	**5.** necklace
collar de perlas	**6.** pearl necklace/pearls
cadena	**7.** chain
collar de cuentas	**8.** beads
prendedor/broche	**9.** pin
reloj/reloj de pulsera	**10.** watch/wrist watch
pulsera/brazalete	**11.** bracelet
gemelos/mancuernas/yuntas	**12.** cuff links

corbata	**13. tie**
pisacorbata/pasador/alfiler de corbata	**14.** tie clip
cinturón/correa	**15.** belt
llavero	**16.** key ring/key chain
billetera	**17.** wallet
monedero	**18.** change purse
cartera/bolso/bolsa para damas	**19.** pocketbook/purse/handbag
carriel/bolso/bolsa para damas/cartera	**20.** shoulder bag
bolso	**21.** tote bag
mochila/bolsa para libros	**22.** book bag
mochila	**23.** backpack
maletín	**24.** briefcase
paraguas/parasol/sombrilla	**25.** umbrella

[In a store]
A. Excuse me. Is this/Are these _____ on sale this week?
B. Yes. It's/They're half price.

[On the street]
A. Help! Police! Stop that man/woman!
B. What happened?!
A. He/She just stole my _____ and my _____!

Do you like to wear jewelry? What jewelry do you have?
In your country, what do men, women, and children use to carry their things?

largo(a) – corto(a)	**1–2** long – short
estrecho(a) – ancho(a)	**3–4** tight – loose/baggy
grande – chico(a)/pequeño(a)	**5–6** large/big – small
alto(a) – bajo(a)	**7–8** high – low
adornado(a)– sencillo(a)	**9–10** fancy – plain
grueso(a) – liviano(a)	**11–12** heavy – light
oscuro(a) – claro(a)	**13–14** dark – light
ancho(a) – angosto(a)/	**15–16** wide – narrow
apretado(a)/estrecho(a)	

rayado(a)/de rayas/de rayitas	**17.** striped
de cuadros/de cuadritos	**18.** checked
diseño a cuadros/madrás	**19.** plaid
punteado(a)/de bolas/de bolitas	**20.** polka dot
estampado(a)	**21.** print
floreado	**22.** flowered
paisley/pesle	**23.** paisley
azul sólido	**24.** solid *blue*

[1–2]
A. Are the sleeves too **long**?
B. No. They're too **short**.

1–2	Are the sleeves too _____?
3–4	Are the pants too _____?
5–6	Are the gloves too _____?
7–8	Are the heels too _____?

9–10	Is the blouse too _____?
11–12	Is the coat too _____?
13–14	Is the color too _____?
15–16	Are the shoes too _____?

[17–24]
A. How do you like this _____ tie/shirt/skirt?
B. Actually, I prefer that _____ one.

Describe your favorite clothing.

EL ALMACÉN

A. Excuse me. Where's the **store directory**?
B. It's over there, next to the **escalator**.

guía/directorio	**1.** (store) directory	(Sección de) Muebles	**14.** Furniture Department/Home Furnishings Department
escalera eléctrica/automática	**2.** escalator		
(Sección de) Ropa de caballeros	**3.** Men's Clothing Department	(Sección de) Electrodomésticos	**15.** Household Appliances Department
Perfumería	**4.** Perfume Counter		
Joyería	**5.** Jewelry Counter	(Sección de) Electrónica	**16.** Electronics Department
ascensor/elevador	**6.** elevator	Mostrador (de) servicio al cliente	**17.** Customer Assistance Counter/Customer Service Counter
servicios/baños para caballeros	**7.** men's room		
servicios/baños para damas	**8.** ladies' room	cafetería/refresquería	**18.** snack bar
fuente de agua	**9.** water fountain	Mostrador de servicio para envolver regalos	**19.** Gift Wrap Counter
estacionamiento/garaje	**10.** parking garage		
(Sección de) Ropa de damas	**11.** Women's Clothing Department	estacionamiento/garaje	**20.** parking lot
(Sección de) Ropa de niños	**12.** Children's Clothing Department	área de recibo	**21.** customer pickup area
(Sección de) Artículos de cocina/Artículos para el hogar	**13.** Housewares Department		

A. Pardon me. Is this the way to the _____?
B. Yes, it is./No, it isn't.

A. I'll meet you at/in/near/in front of the _____.
B. Okay. What time?
A. At *3:00.*

Describe a department store you know. Tell what is on each floor.

A. May I help you?
B. Yes, please. I'm looking for a **TV**.

televisor/televisión	**1.** TV/television set	equipo estereofónico/de estéreo/ **13.** stereo system/sound system
control remoto	**2.** remote control (unit)	equipo de sonido
videocasetera/videograbadora/	**3.** VCR/videocassette recorder	grabadora de cintas/ **14.** tape recorder
videoreproductora		grabadora de cintas
videocinta/videocasete en blanco	**4.** (blank) videotape	magnetofónicas
videocinta/videocasete	**5.** video/(video)tape	casetera personal/Walkman **15.** (personal) cassette player/
videofilmadora/videocámara/	**6.** camcorder/video camera	Walkman
cámara de video		tocacasetera/tocacintas/ **16.** portable stereo system/
tornamesa/giradiscos/	**7.** turntable	equipo estereofónico portátil boom box
plato giratorio		audiocinta/audiocasete **17.** (audio) tape/(audio) cassette
casetera	**8.** tape deck	CD/disco compacto **18.** CD/compact disc
tocador de discos compactos	**9.** CD player/compact disc player	disco **19.** record
amplificador	**10.** amplifier	audífonos/auriculares **20.** set of headphones
sintonizador	**11.** tuner	radio **21.** radio
bocina	**12.** speaker	radio de onda corta **22.** shortwave radio
		radio reloj/despertador **23.** clock radio

A. How do you like my _____?
B. It's great/fantastic/awesome!

A. Which company makes a good _____?
B. In my opinion, the best _____ is made by ....

What video and audio equipment do you have or want?
In your opinion, which brands are the best?

A. Can you recommend a good **computer**?*
B. Yes. This **computer** here is excellent.

With 9, use: Can you recommend good _____?

computadora/	**1.** computer	transmisor-receptor (de documentos)	**15.** fax machine
ordenador de escritorio		electrónico inmediato/fax	
monitor	**2.** monitor	cámara	**16.** camera
unidad base	**3.** disk drive	visor/lente zoom	**17.** zoom lens
teclado	**4.** keyboard	estuche de la cámara	**18.** camera case
ratón	**5.** mouse	accesorio de luz relámpago/de flash	**19.** flash attachment
impresora	**6.** printer	trípode	**20.** tripod
comunicador telefónico/	**7.** modem	película/film	**21.** film
teleprocesador		proyector de transparencias/	**22.** slide projector
disco/disco blando/disquete	**8.** (floppy) disk/diskette	diapositivas	
programas y procedimientos	**9.** (computer) software	pantalla	**23.** (movie) screen
computadora/ordenador portátil	**10.** portable computer	máquina de escribir eléctrica	**24.** electric typewriter
computadora portátil ligera/	**11.** notebook computer	máquina de escribir electrónica	**25.** electronic typewriter
ordenador portátil ligero		calculadora	**26.** calculator
teléfono	**12.** telephone/phone	máquina de sumar/sumadora	**27.** adding machine
radioteléfono/teléfono portátil	**13.** portable phone/portable telephone	transformador	**28.** voltage regulator
contestador(a) automático(a)	**14.** answering machine	adaptador de corriente	**29.** adapter

A. Excuse me. Do you sell
_____s?†

B. Yes. We carry a complete line of
_____s.†

†With 9 and 21, use the singular.

A. Which _____ is the best?
B. This one here. It's made by
....

Do you have a camera? What kind
is it? What do you take pictures of?
Does anyone you know have an
answering machine? When you
call, what does the machine say?
How have computers changed the world?

A. Excuse me. I'm looking for (a/an) _____(s) for my *grandson*.*
B. Look in the next aisle.
A. Thank you.

* *grandson/granddaughter/…*

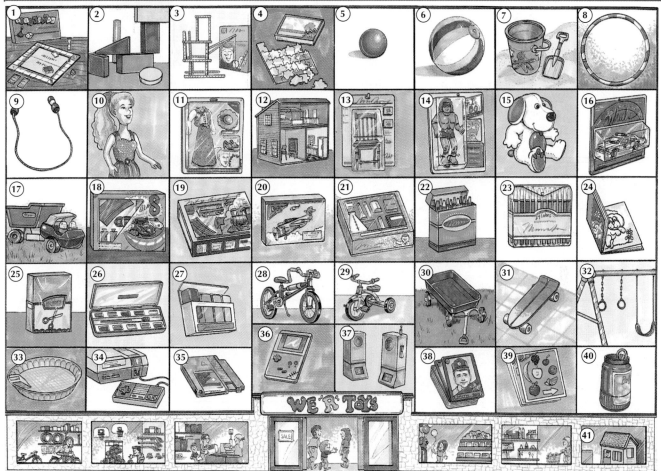

juego/	**1.** (board) game	carrito de juguete	**16.** matchbox car
juego de tablero		camión de juguete/troquita	**17.** toy truck
cubitos/bloques	**2.** (building) blocks	juego de carros de carrera	**18.** racing car set
juguete para armar/	**3.** construction	juego de trenes	**19.** train set
juego de Meccano	set	juego de maqueta/	**20.** model kit
rompecabezas	**4.** (jigsaw) puzzle	modelo para armar	
bola de caucho/	**5.** rubber ball	juego de laboratorio/	**21.** science kit
de goma		de química	
pelota/bola	**6.** beach ball	lápices de cera/	**22.** crayons
de playa/balón		crayones/crayolas	
cubito y palita	**7.** pail and shovel	marcadores/	**23.** (color) markers
aro/hula hoop	**8.** hula hoop	lápices de felpa	
soga/cuerda	**9.** jump rope	libro/cuaderno de dibujos/	**24.** coloring book
muñeca	**10.** doll	de pintar/para colerear	
ropa de muñeca	**11.** doll clothing	papel de construcción	**25.** construction
casa de muñecas	**12.** doll house		paper
muebles para	**13.** doll house	juego de pintura	**26.** paint set
la casa de muñecas	furniture	masilla/arcilla/plasticina	**27.** (modeling) clay
figura mecánica	**14.** action figure	bicicleta	**28.** bicycle
peluche	**15.** stuffed animal	triciclo	**29.** tricycle

vagón	**30.** wagon
patín/patineta	**31.** skateboard
columpio	**32.** swing set
piscina infantil/	**33.** plastic swimming
chapoteadero(a)	pool/wading pool
consola/sistema	**34.** video game system
de videojuego	
cartucho/paquete	**35.** (video) game
de videojuego	cartridge
videojuego manual	**36.** hand-held
	video game
intercomunicador/	**37.** walkie-talkie (set)
talkie-walki/	
walki talki	
figuritas	**38.** trading cards
calcomanías/	**39.** stickers
pegatinas de colores	
pompas de jabón/	**40.** bubble soap
burbujas de jabón	
casa de jugar	**41.** play house

A. I don't know what to get my
...........-year-old son/daughter
for his/her birthday.
B. What about (a) _____?

A. Mom/Dad? Can we buy
this/these _____?
B. No, *Johnny*. Not today.

What toys are most popular in your
country?
What were your favorite toys when
you were a child?

EL DINERO

Monedas/Coins

	Name	Value	Written as:	
1.	penny	one cent	1¢	$ .01
2.	nickel	five cents	5¢	$ .05
3.	dime	ten cents	10¢	$ .10
4.	quarter	twenty-five cents	25¢	$ .25
5.	half dollar	fifty cents	50¢	$ .50
6.	silver dollar	one dollar		$1.00

A. How much is a **penny** worth?
B. A penny is worth **one cent**.

A. *Soda* costs *seventy-five cents*.
    Do you have enough change?
B. Yes. I have a/two/three _____(s) and . . . .

Monedas/Currency

	Name	We sometimes say:	Value	Written as:
7.	(one-)dollar bill	a one	one dollar	$ 1.00
8.	five-dollar bill	a five	five dollars	$ 5.00
9.	ten-dollar bill	a ten	ten dollars	$ 10.00
10.	twenty-dollar bill	a twenty	twenty dollars	$ 20.00
11.	fifty-dollar bill	a fifty	fifty dollars	$ 50.00
12.	(one-)hundred dollar bill	a hundred	one hundred dollars	$100.00

A. I need to go to the supermarket.
    Do you have any cash?
B. Let me see. I have a **twenty-dollar bill**.
A. **Twenty dollars** is enough. Thanks.

A. Can you change a **five-dollar bill/a five**?
B. Yes. I've got *five* **one-dollar bills**/*five ones*.

Written as	We say:
$1.20	one dollar and twenty cents
	a dollar twenty
$2.50	two dollars and fifty cents
	two fifty
$37.43	thirty-seven dollars and forty-three cents
	thirty-seven forty-three

How much do you pay for a loaf of bread? a hamburger?
    a cup of coffee? a gallon of gas?
Name and describe the coins and currency in your country.
    What are they worth in U.S. dollars?

chequera/talonario de cheques	**1.** checkbook	
registro de cheques	**2.** check register	
estado de cuenta	**3.** monthly statement	
libreta de banco	**4.** bank book	
cheques de viajero/viajeros	**5.** traveler's checks	
tarjeta de crédito	**6.** credit card	
cajero automático	**7.** ATM card	
comprobante de depósito	**8.** deposit slip	
comprobante de retiro	**9.** withdrawal slip	
cheque	**10.** check	

giro postal/orden monetaria	**11.** money order
formulario para solicitud de préstamos	**12.** loan application
caja/bóveda	**13.** (bank) vault
caja de seguridad	**14.** safe deposit box
cajero/cajera/operador bancario	**15.** teller
guarda/guardia de seguridad	**16.** security guard
cajero automático	**17.** automatic teller (machine)/ ATM (machine)
supervisor/ ejecutivo de banco	**18.** bank officer

[1–7]
A. What are you looking for?
B. My _____. I can't find it/them anywhere!

[8–12]
A. What are you doing?
B. I'm filling out this _____.
A. For how much?
B. ....

[13–18]
A. How many _____s does the State Street Bank have?
B. ....

Do you have a bank account? What kind? Where?
Do you ever use traveler's checks? When?
Do you have a credit card? What kind? When do you use it?

EL CUERPO HUMANO

[1–23, 27–79]

A. My doctor checked my **head** and said everything is okay.

B. I'm glad to hear that.

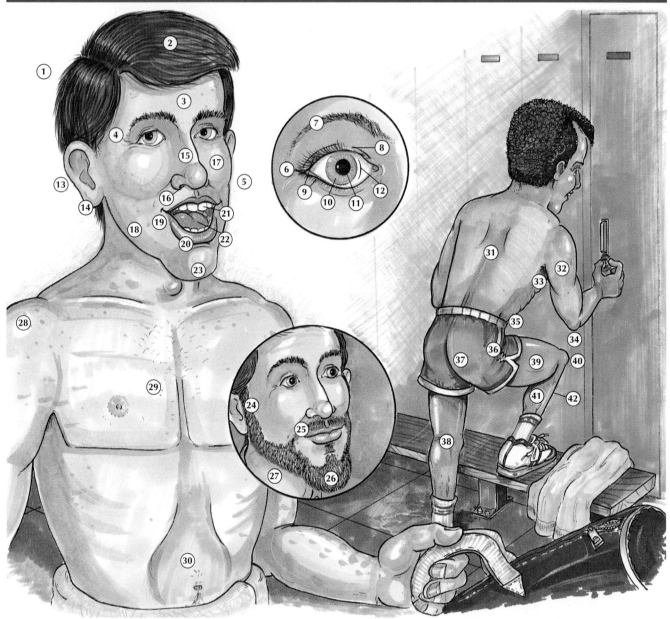

cabeza	**1.** head	ventanilla de la nariz/	**16.** nostril		estómago	**30.** abdomen
cabello/pelo	**2.** hair	ventana de la nariz/narices			espalda	**31.** back
frente	**3.** forehead	mejilla/pómulo	**17.** cheek		brazo	**32.** arm
sien	**4.** temple	quijada	**18.** jaw		axila/sobaco	**33.** armpit
cara	**5.** face	boca	**19.** mouth		codo	**34.** elbow
ojo	**6.** eye	labio	**20.** lip		cintura	**35.** waist
ceja	**7.** eyebrow	diente-dientes	**21.** tooth–teeth		cadera	**36.** hip
párpado	**8.** eyelid	lengua	**22.** tongue		nalgas	**37.** buttocks
pestañas	**9.** eyelashes	mentón/barbilla	**23.** chin		pierna	**38.** leg
iris	**10.** iris	patillas	**24.** sideburn		muslo	**39.** thigh
pupila	**11.** pupil	bigote/mostacho	**25.** mustache		rodilla	**40.** knee
córnea	**12.** cornea	barba	**26.** beard		pantorrilla	**41.** calf
oreja/oído	**13.** ear	cuello	**27.** neck		espinilla	**42.** shin
lóbulo	**14.** earlobe	hombro	**28.** shoulder			
nariz	**15.** nose	pecho	**29.** chest			

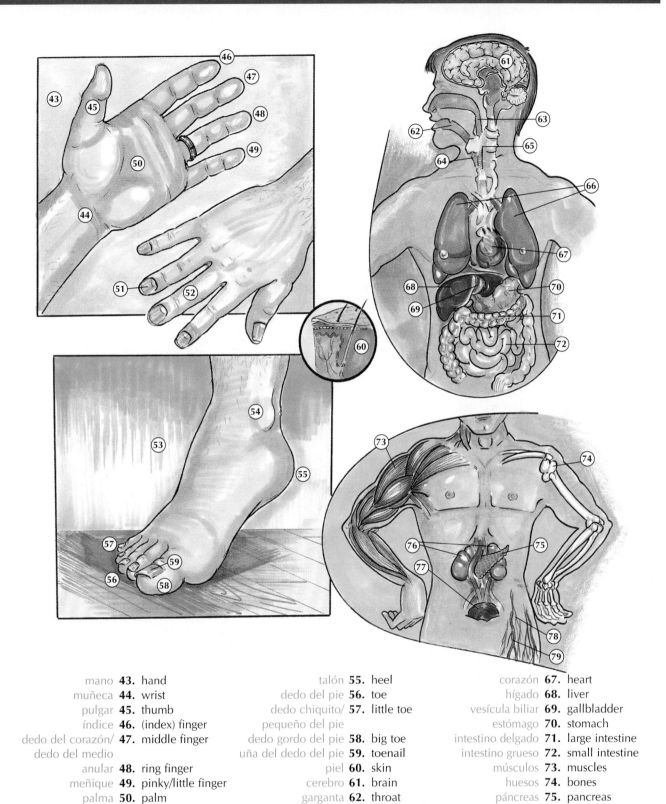

mano	**43.**	hand	talón	**55.**	heel	corazón	**67.** heart
muñeca	**44.**	wrist	dedo del pie	**56.**	toe	hígado	**68.** liver
pulgar	**45.**	thumb	dedo chiquito/	**57.**	little toe	vesícula biliar	**69.** gallbladder
índice	**46.**	(index) finger	pequeño del pie			estómago	**70.** stomach
dedo del corazón/	**47.**	middle finger	dedo gordo del pie	**58.**	big toe	intestino delgado	**71.** large intestine
dedo del medio			uña del dedo del pie	**59.**	toenail	intestino grueso	**72.** small intestine
anular	**48.**	ring finger	piel	**60.**	skin	músculos	**73.** muscles
meñique	**49.**	pinky/little finger	cerebro	**61.**	brain	huesos	**74.** bones
palma	**50.**	palm	garganta	**62.**	throat	páncreas	**75.** pancreas
uña	**51.**	fingernail	esófago	**63.**	esophagus	riñones	**76.** kidneys
nudillo	**52.**	knuckle	tráquea	**64.**	windpipe	vejiga	**77.** bladder
pie	**53.**	foot	médula espinal	**65.**	spinal cord	venas	**78.** veins
tobillo	**54.**	ankle	pulmones	**66.**	lungs	arterias	**79.** arteries

[1, 3–8, 13–23, 27–34, 36–60]

A. Ooh!

B. What's the matter?

A. { My _____ hurts!
{ My _____ s hurt!

[61–79]

A. My doctor wants me to have some tests.

B. Why?

A. She's concerned about my _____.

Describe yourself as completely as you can.

Which parts of the body are most important at school? at work? when you play your favorite sport?

MALESTARES, SÍNTOMAS, LESIONES Y ENFERMEDADES

A. What's the matter?
B. I have a/an [1–19] .

A. What's the matter?
B. I have [20–26] .

dolor de cabeza	**1.** headache	tos	**9.** cough	verruga	**19.** wart
dolor de oído	**2.** earache	virus	**10.** virus	hipo	**20.** (the) hiccups
dolor de muelas	**3.** toothache	infección	**11.** infection	escalofrío	**21.** (the) chills
dolor de estómago	**4.** stomachache	salpullido/sarpullido	**12.** rash	calambre	**22.** cramps
dolor de espaldas	**5.** backache	picada/picadura	**13.** insect bite	diarrea	**23.** diarrhea
dolor/ardor de garganta/	**6.** sore throat	quemadura de sol	**14.** sunburn	dolor en el pecho	**24.** chest pain
garganta inflamada		tortícolis	**15.** stiff neck	jadeo	**25.** shortness of
fiebre/calentura	**7.** fever/temperature	moqueo	**16.** runny nose		breath
gripe/resfriado/	**8.** cold	hemorragia nasal	**17.** bloody nose	laringitis	**26.** laryngitis
catarro/trancazo		carie	**18.** cavity		

A. What's the matter?
B. { I feel __[27–30]__ .
     { I'm __[31–32]__ .
     { I'm __[33–38]__ ing.

A. What's the matter?
B. { I __[39–48]__ ed my ....
     { My .... is/are __[49–50]__ .

desmayo **27.** faint	respirar con dificultad **35.** wheeze	rasparse/rasguñarse **43.** scrape
mareo **28.** dizzy	eructar **36.** burp	magullarse/golpearse **44.** bruise
náusea **29.** nauseous	vomitar/arrojar **37.** vomit/throw up	quemarse **45.** burn
hinchado (a) **30.** bloated	sangrar **38.** bleed	romperse **46.** break–broke
congestionado (a) **31.** congested	torcerse/retorcerse **39.** twist	golpearse/lastimarse **47.** hurt–hurt
agotado (a) **32.** exhausted	torcerse **40.** sprain	cortarse **48.** cut–cut
toser **33.** cough	dislocarse **41.** dislocate	inchado **49.** swollen
estornudar **34.** sneeze	arañarse **42.** scratch	picar **50.** itch

A. How do you feel?
B. Not so good./Not very well./Terrible!
A. What's the matter?
B. ...., ..., and ....
A. I'm sorry to hear that.

Tell about the last time you didn't feel well. What was the matter?
Tell about a time you hurt yourself. What happened? How?
What are the symptoms of a cold? a heart problem?

CUIDADO MÉDICO Y DENTAL

médico/doctor(a)	**1.** doctor/physician	
enfermera(o)	**2.** nurse	
radiólogo	**3.** X-ray technician	
técnico de laboratorio	**4.** lab technician	
paramédico	**5.** EMT/emergency medical technician	
dentista	**6.** dentist	
higienista	**7.** (oral) hygienist	
obstetra	**8.** obstetrician	
ginecólogo	**9.** gynecologist	
pediatra	**10.** pediatrician	
cardiólogo	**11.** cardiologist	

oculista	**12.** optometrist	
cirujano	**13.** surgeon	
psiquiatra	**14.** psychiatrist	
camilla de examen/ mesa de reconocimiento	**15.** examination table	
cartilla para medir la visión/cartilla de SNEM	**16.** eye chart	
pesa	**17.** scale	
máquina de rayos X (equis)/ máquina de radiografías	**18.** X-ray machine	
estetoscopio	**19.** stethoscope	
termómetro	**20.** thermometer	

guantes	**21.** gloves	
esfigomanómetro/ esfigmómetro	**22.** blood pressure gauge	
aguja/jeringa/ jeringilla	**23.** needle/syringe	
gasa/venda/vendaje	**24.** bandages/gauze	
esparadrapo	**25.** adhesive tape	
alcohol	**26.** alcohol	
motas de algodón	**27.** cotton balls	
taladro	**28.** drill	
anestesia/novocaína	**29.** anesthetic/ Novocaine	

[1–14]
A. What do you do?
B. I'm a/an _____.

[15–18]
A. Please step over here to the _____.
B. Okay.

[19–29]
A. Please hand me the _____.
B. Here you are.

Where do you go for medical care? How often? Who examines you? What does he/she do?

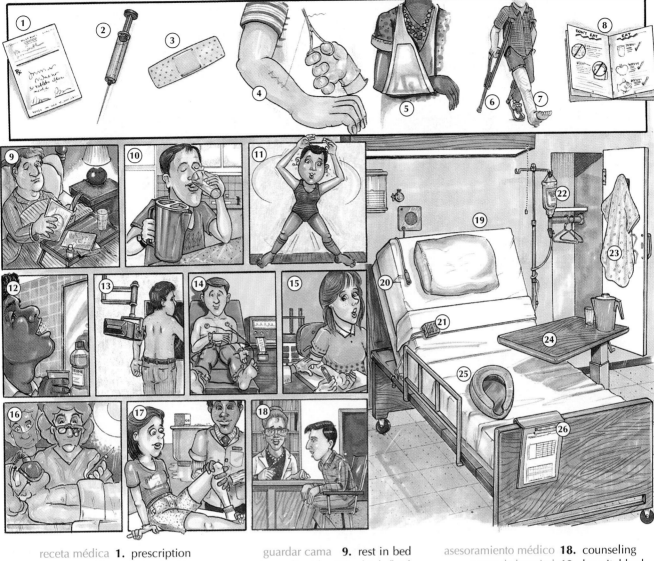

Spanish		English	Spanish		English	Spanish		English
receta médica	**1.**	prescription	guardar cama	**9.**	rest in bed	asesoramiento médico	**18.**	counseling
inyección	**2.**	injection/shot	tomar líquidos	**10.**	drink fluids	cama de hospital	**19.**	hospital bed
curita/tirita/	**3.**	bandaid	hacer ejercicios	**11.**	exercise	timbre	**20.**	call button
parche/venda			hacer gárgaras	**12.**	gargle	control de la cama	**21.**	bed control
puntos	**4.**	stitches	radiografías/rayos X (equis)	**13.**	X-rays	venoclisis/intravenosa	**22.**	I.V.
cabestrillo	**5.**	sling	análisis/pruebas	**14.**	tests	bata de hospital	**23.**	hospital gown
muletas	**6.**	crutches	análsis/pruebas de sangre	**15.**	blood work/	mesa	**24.**	bed table
yeso/enyesado/	**7.**	cast			blood tests	paleta/cuña	**25.**	bed pan
escayola			operación	**16.**	surgery	cuadrícula/hoja clínica	**26.**	medical chart
dieta/régimen	**8.**	diet	fisioterapia	**17.**	physical therapy			

[1–8]
A. What did the doctor do?
B. She/He gave me (a/an) _____.

[9–18]
A. What did the doctor say?
B. { She/He told me to [9–12].
{ She/He told me I need [13–18].

[19–26]
A. This is your _____.
B. I see.

When did you have your last medical checkup?
What did the doctor say?

Have you ever been in the hospital?
When? Why? Tell about your experience.

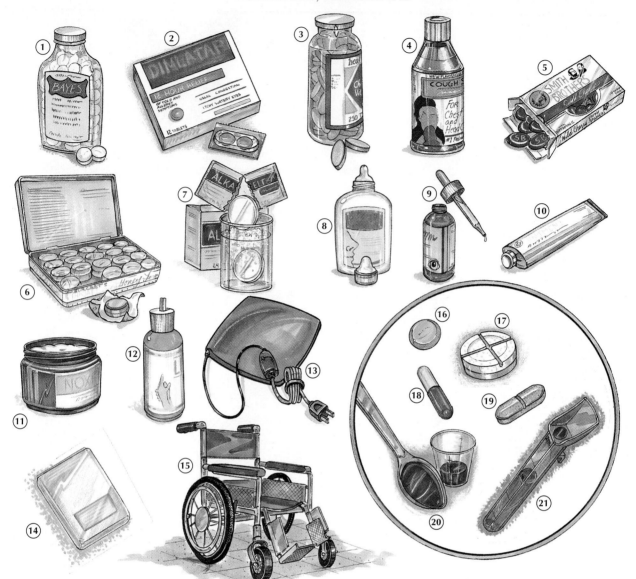

aspirina	**1.** aspirin	antiácido/tabletas para la	**7.** antacid tablets	silla de ruedas	**15.** wheelchair
pastillas/píldoras	**2.** cold tablets	acidez estomacal		píldora	**16.** pill
para la gripe/		descongestionante nasal	**8.** decongestant	pastilla/tableta	**17.** tablet
el resfriado/el catarro		(en atomizador)	spray/nasal spray	cápsula	**18.** capsule
vitaminas	**3.** vitamins	gota para los ojos	**9.** eye drops	cápsula comprimida/	**19.** caplet
jarabe para la tos	**4.** cough syrup	ungüento	**10.** ointment	capeleta	
pastillas para la tos	**5.** cough drops	crema/pomada	**11.** creme	cucharadita	**20.** teaspoon
pastillas para la garganta	**6.** throat lozenges	loción	**12.** lotion	cucharada	**21.** tablespoon
		parche caliente	**13.** heating pad		
		bolsa de hielo	**14.** ice pack		

[1–15] A. What did the doctor say?

B. { She/He told me to take [1–4] .
      { She/He told me to use (a/an) [5–15] .

[16–21] A. What's the dosage?

B. One _____, every three hours.

What medicines do you take or use?
For what ailments?

Describe any medical treatments or medicines in your
country that are different from the ones in these lessons.

EL CORREO

carta	**1.**	letter	pliego de estampillas/ de sellos	**12.**	sheet of stamps	
tarjeta postal	**2.**	postcard	rollo de estampillas/ de sellos	**13.**	roll of stamps	
aerograma	**3.**	air letter/ aerogramme	libreta/carterita de estampillas/de sellos	**14.**	book of stamps	

estampilla **22.** stamp/postage
sello de correos/ **23.** postmark
sello postal
buzón **24.** mail slot
ventanilla **25.** window
empleado de correos **26.** postal worker/ postal clerk

carta **1.** letter
tarjeta postal **2.** postcard
aerograma **3.** air letter/ aerogramme
paquete postal **4.** package/parcel
primera clase **5.** first class
correo aéreo **6.** air mail
paquete postal **7.** parcel post
impresos/ **8.** book rate/
tercera clase third class
certificado **9.** registered mail
urgente/entrega **10.** express mail/
inmediata/expreso overnight mail
estampilla/sello **11.** stamp

pliego de estampillas/ **12.** sheet of stamps
de sellos
rollo de estampillas/ **13.** roll of stamps
de sellos
libreta/carterita de **14.** book of stamps
estampillas/de sellos
giro postal/ **15.** money order
orden monetaria
formulario de cambio **16.** change-of-address
de dirección form
solicitud para servicio **17.** selective service
selectivo registration form
sobre **18.** envelope
dirección **19.** address
código/área postal **20.** zip code
remitente/señas del **21.** return address
remitente

estampilla **22.** stamp/postage
sello de correos/ **23.** postmark
sello postal
buzón **24.** mail slot
ventanilla **25.** window
empleado de correos **26.** postal worker/
postal clerk
balanza/pesa **27.** scale
máquinilla de **28.** stamp machine
estampillas/de sellos
camión de correos **29.** mail truck
buzón **30.** mailbox
cartero(a) **31.** letter carrier/
mail carrier
bolsa de correo/ **32.** mail bag
portacartas

[1–4]
A. Where are you going?
B. To the post office.
I have to mail a/an _____.

[11–17]
A. Next!
B. I'd like a _____, please.
A. Here you are.

[5–10]
A. How do you want
to send it?
B. _____, please.

[19–22]
A. Do you want me to
mail this letter for you?
B. Yes, thanks.
A. Oops! You forgot the
_____!

What time does your letter carrier
deliver your mail? Does he/she drive a
mail truck or carry a mail bag and walk?

Describe the post office you use:
How many postal windows are there?
Is there a stamp machine?
Are the postal workers friendly?

Tell about the postal system in your
country.

bibliotecario(a)	**1.** librarian	fotocopiadora/sacacopias/	**10.** copier/(photo)copy	sección de revistas	**21.** periodicals
recepción/	**2.** checkout desk	máquina de xerox	machine		section
mostrador de chequeo		bibliotecaria de la sección	**11.** reference librarian	periódico	**22.** newspaper
ayudante	**3.** library assistant	de referencias		revista	**23.** magazine
microfilm	**4.** microfilm	sección de referencias	**12.** reference section	boletín informativo	**24.** journal
microficha	**5.** microfiche	atlas	**13.** atlas	ficha/tarjeta	**25.** call card
catálogo/tarjetero/fichero	**6.** card catalog	enciclopedia	**14.** encyclopedia	número de clasificación	**26.** call number
catálogo computa-	**7.** online catalog	diccionario	**15.** dictionary	autor	**27.** author
dorizado/catálogo acce-		centro audiovisual	**16.** media section	título	**28.** title
sible con computadora		video/videocinta	**17.** videotape	materia	**29.** subject
estantería/librero(a)/	**8.** shelves	disco	**18.** record	carnet/tarjeta	**30.** library card
anaqueles/tablillas		cinta adhesiva	**19.** tape	de identificación	
información	**9.** information desk	disco blando/diskette	**20.** computer diskette		

[1–11]

A. Excuse me. Where's/
   Where are the _____?

B. Over there, at/near/next to
   the _____.

[12–24]

A. Excuse me. Where can I find
   a/an _[13–15, 17–20, 22–24]_ ?

B. Look in the _[12, 16, 21]_ over
   there.

[27–29]

A. May I help you?

B. Yes, please. I'm having
   trouble finding a book.

A. Do you know the _____?

B. Yes. ....

Do you go to a library? Which one? What does this library have? Describe how you use the library.

oficina	**1.** office	laboratorio de química	**9.** chemistry lab	subdirector(a)	**18.** assistant principal
enfermería	**2.** nurse's office	salón/sala	**10.** teachers' lounge	enfermero(a)	**19.** (school) nurse
consejería	**3.** guidance office	de profesores		consejero(a)	**20.** guidance counselor
cafetería	**4.** cafeteria	gimnasio	**11.** gym/gymnasium	supervisor/inspector	**21.** lunchroom monitor
dirección	**5.** principal's office	vestidor/vestidores	**12.** locker room	de la cafetería	
salón/sala	**6.** classroom	auditorio	**13.** auditorium	empleado(a)	**22.** cafeteria worker
de clases/aula		campo de juego	**14.** field	de la cafetería	
casillero	**7.** locker	gradería/gradas/bancas	**15.** bleachers	maestro(a) de manejo/	**23.** driver's ed instructor
laboratorio	**8.** language lab	pista/cancha	**16.** track	de conducir	
de lenguas		director (a)	**17.** principal	maestro(a)	**24.** teacher
				entrenador(a)	**25.** coach
				portero(a)/conserje	**26.** custodian

[1–16] A. Where are you going?

B. I'm going to the _____.*

A. Do you have a hall pass?

B. Yes. Here it is.

With 6 and 7, use: I'm going to my _____.

[17–26] A. Who's that?

B. That's the new

Describe the school where you study English.
Tell about the rooms, offices, and people.

Tell about differences between schools in the United States
and in your country.

CURSOS/MATERIAS Y ACTIVIDADES EXTRACURRICULARES

  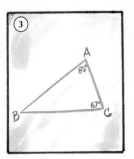  

  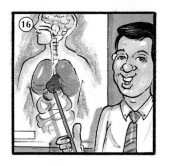 

matemáticas	**1.** math/mathematics	ciencias	**9.** science	taller de artes y oficios/	**17.** industrial arts/shop
álgebra	**2.** algebra	biología	**10.** biology	de artes industriales	
geometría	**3.** geometry	química	**11.** chemistry	curso de manejo/	**18.** driver's education/
trigonometría	**4.** trigonometry	física	**12.** physics	de conducir	driver's ed
cálculo	**5.** calculus	español	**13.** Spanish	mecanografía	**19.** typing
inglés	**6.** English	francés	**14.** French	arte	**20.** art
historia	**7.** history	economía doméstica	**15.** home economics	música	**21.** music
geografía	**8.** geography	higiene	**16.** health		

banda	**22.** band	periódico estudiantil	**27.** school newspaper
orquesta	**23.** orchestra	anuario	**28.** yearbook
coro	**24.** choir/chorus	revista literaria	**29.** literary magazine
drama/teatro	**25.** drama	asociación de estudiantes	**30.** student government
fútbol americano	**26.** football		

[1–21]
A. What do you have next period?
B. _____. How about you?
A. _____.
B. There's the bell. I've got to go.

[22–30]
A. Are you going home right after school?
B. { No. I have __[22–26]__ practice.
    { No. I have a __[27–30]__ meeting.

What is/was your favorite subject? Why? What extracurricular activities do/did you participate in?

PROFESIONES Y OFICIOS I

A. What do you do?
B. I'm an **accountant**. How about you?
A. I'm a **carpenter**.

contable/contador	**1.** accountant	montador(a)	**6.** assembler	busero(a)/conductor/	**11.** bus driver
actor	**2.** actor	panadero(a)	**7.** baker	chofer de autobús	
actriz	**3.** actress	barbero(a)	**8.** barber	carnicero(a)	**12.** butcher
arquitecto(a)	**4.** architect	tenedor(a) de libros/	**9.** bookkeeper	carpintero(a)	**13.** carpenter
artista	**5.** artist	contador(a)		cajero(a)	**14.** cashier
		albañil	**10.** bricklayer/mason	chef/cocinero(a)	**15.** chef/cook

programador(a)	**16.** computer programmer	repartidor	**21.** delivery person	maestro de obras/	**26.** foreman
obrero(a)	**17.** construction worker	electricista	**22.** electrician	capataz	
mensajero	**18.** courier/messenger	granjero/agricultor/	**23.** farmer	jardinero(a)	**27.** gardener
portero(a)/conserje	**19.** custodian/janitor	hacendado		peluquero(a)	**28.** hairdresser
operador(a) en	**20.** data processor	bombero	**24.** firefighter	ama de casa	**29.** housekeeper
computación e informática		pescador	**25.** fisherman	periodista/reportero(a)	**30.** journalist/reporter

[At a job interview]
A. Are you an experienced _____?
B. Yes. I'm a very experienced _____.

A. How long have you been a/an _____?
B. I've been a/an _____ for .... months/years.

Which of these occupations do you think are the most interesting? the most difficult? Why?

PROFESIONES Y OFICIOS II

A. What's your occupation?
B. I'm a **lawyer**.
A. A **lawyer**?
B. Yes. That's right.

abogado(a)	**1.** lawyer	boticario/farmacéu- **6.** pharmacist	vendedor(a)/agente de bienes raíces **11.** real estate agent
mecánico(a)	**2.** mechanic	tico(a)/farmacista	recepcionista/recepcionista-telefonista **12.** receptionist
modelo	**3.** model	fotógrafo(a) **7.** photographer	ayudante **13.** repairperson
locutor(a)/	**4.** newscaster	piloto(a) **8.** pilot	vendedor(a) **14.** salesperson
reportero(a)		plomero(a) **9.** plumber	empleado del departamento **15.** sanitation worker
pintor(a)	**5.** painter	policía **10.** police officer	de salubridad

científico(a)	**16.** scientist	
costurero(a)	**17.** seamstress	
secretario(a)	**18.** secretary	
guarda/guardia de seguridad	**19.** security guard	
empleado(a) (del depósito)	**20.** stock clerk	

sastre	**21.** tailor	
taxista	**22.** taxi driver	
maestro(a)	**23.** teacher	
traductor(a)/ intérprete	**24.** translator/ interpreter	
agente de viajes	**25.** travel agent	

camionero(a)	**26.** truck driver	
camarero/mesero/mozo(a)	**27.** waiter	
camarera/mesera	**28.** waitress	
soldador(a)	**29.** welder	
veterinario(a)	**30.** veterinarian	

A. Are you still a _____?
B. No. I'm a _____.
A. Oh. That's interesting.

A. What kind of job would you like in the future?
B. I'd like to be a _____.

Do you work? What's your occupation?
What are the occupations of people in your family?

ACTIVIDADES RELACIONADAS CON EL TRABAJO

A. Can you **act**?
B. Yes, I can.

actuar	**1.** act	
armar *componentes*/	**2.** assemble	
montar *componentes*	*components*	
hornear	**3.** bake	
hacer *cosas*/	**4.** build *things*/	
construir *cosas*	construct *things*	
limpiar	**5.** clean	
cocinar	**6.** cook	
repartir *pizzas*	**7.** deliver *pizzas*	
diseñar *edificios*	**8.** design *buildings*	
dibujar	**9.** draw	
conducir/manejar	**10.** drive *a truck*	
un camión		
archivar	**11.** file	
volar *un avión*	**12.** fly *an airplane*	
sembrar vegetales	**13.** grow	
	vegetables	
vigilar *edificios*/	**14.** guard	
cuidar *edificios*	*buildings*	

cortar *el césped/la grama/el zacate*	**15.** mow *lawns*	
manejar *herramientas/máquinas/*	**16.** operate *equipment*	
operar *herramientas/máquinas*		
pintar	**17.** paint	
tocar *el piano*	**18.** play the *piano*	
arreglar/componer *cosas*	**19.** repair *things*/fix *things*	
vender *autos/carros*	**20.** sell *cars*	

servir *comida*	**21.** serve *food*
coser	**22.** sew
cantar	**23.** sing
enseñar	**24.** teach
traducir	**25.** translate
escribir *a máquina*	**26.** type
lavar *platos*	**27.** wash *dishes*
escribir	**28.** write

A. What do you do for a living?
B. I _____.

A. Do you know how to _____?
B. Yes. I've been _____ing for years.

Tell about your work abilities.
What can you do?

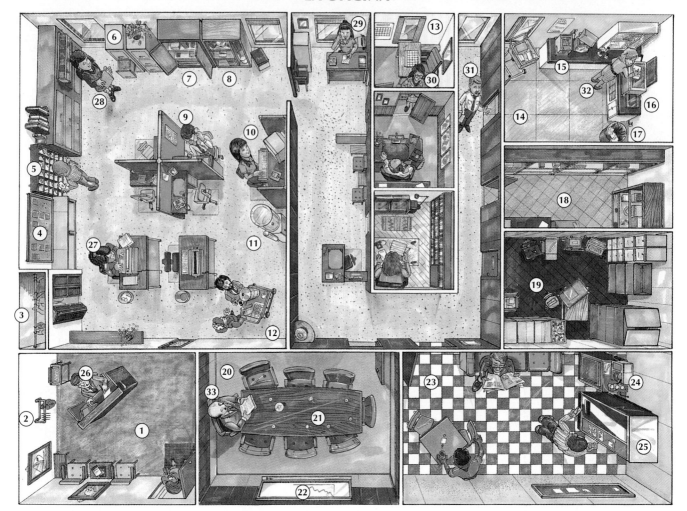

recepción	**1.** reception area		papelera/cesto	**17.** waste receptacle
perchero	**2.** coat rack		cuarto de materiales	**18.** supply room
ropero	**3.** coat closet		depósito	**19.** storage room
tablero (de anuncios)	**4.** message board		sala de conferencias	**20.** conference room
buzón	**5.** mailbox		mesa de reuniones/	**21.** conference table
archivador	**6.** file cabinet		de conferencias	
gabinete/estante	**7.** supply cabinet		cartelera/tablero/tablón/	**22.** whiteboard/dry
gabinete/estante de almacenaje	**8.** storage cabinet		mural de anuncios	erase board
área/módulo/	**9.** workstation		salón/sala de empleados	**23.** employee lounge
estación de trabajo			cafetera eléctrica	**24.** coffee machine
estación/módulo de la computadora	**10.** computer workstation		dispensadora de sodas/	**25.** soda machine
fuente	**11.** water cooler		máquina de sodas	
carrito del café	**12.** coffee cart		recepcionista	**26.** receptionist
oficina	**13.** office		mecanógrafa	**27.** typist
cuarto del correo	**14.** mailroom		archivero(a)/archivista	**28.** file clerk
máquina de sellos/	**15.** postage machine/		secretario(a)	**29.** secretary
estampillas	postage meter		asistente del gerente	**30.** administrative assistant
fotocopiadora/copiadora	**16.** copier/(photo)copy machine		gerente/administrador	**31.** office manager
			auxiliar/asistente	**32.** office assistant
			jefe	**33.** employer/boss

[1–25] A. Where's ....?

B { He's/She's in the/his/her _____.*
    He's/She's at the/his/her _____.†

*1, 13, 14, 18–20, 23   †2–12, 15–17, 21, 22, 24, 25

[26–33] A. Who's he/she?

B. He's/She's the new _____.

EQUIPO DE OFICINA

A. Do you know how to work this **computer**?
B. No, I don't.
A. Let me show you how.

computadora/ ordenadora	**1.** computer	procesador de palabras	**6.** word processor	transmisor-receptor (de documentos)	**15.** fax machine
terminal	**2.** VDT/video display terminal	máquina de escribir calculadora	**7.** typewriter **8.** calculator	electrónico inmediato/fax sacapuntas	**16.** pencil sharpener
impresora con mecanismo de máquina de escribir	**3.** (dot-matrix) printer	calculadora/sumadora grabadora/ dictáfono	**9.** adding machine **10.** microcassette recorder/dictaphone	sacapuntas eléctrico guillotina	**17.** electric pencil sharpener **18.** paper cutter
impresora de alta calidad	**4.** (letter-quality) printer	teléfono audífono	**11.** telephone **12.** headset	sella-plásticos/ sellador(a) de plásticos	**19.** plastic binding machine
impresora laser	**5.** (laser) printer	centralita (máquina) télex	**13.** phone system **14.** telex machine	pesa/balanza trituradora de papel	**20.** postal scale **21.** paper shredder

A. I think this _____ is broken!
B. I'll take a look at it.

A. Have you seen the new _____?
B. No, I haven't.
A. It's much better than the old one!

Do you know how to operate a computer? a fax machine? Give step-by-step instructions for using some type of office equipment.

escritorio	**1.** desk	horario/planificador	**14.** wall planner	cheque	**25.** paycheck
silla giratoria	**2.** swivel chair	archivador	**15.** file cabinet	abrecartas/cortaplumas	**26.** letter opener
rolodex/ fichero/agenda	**3.** rolodex	(en)grapadora	**16.** stapler	tijeras	**27.** scissors
lapicero	**4.** pencil cup	desengrapador(a)	**17.** staple remover	perforadora/	**28.** punch
bandeja tamaño carta/	**5.** letter tray/	dispensador de cinta	**18.** tape dispenser	ponchadora	
apilable	stacking tray	pegante/adhesiva		perforadora/ponchadora	**29.** 3-hole punch
portamemo	**6.** memo holder	dispensador de	**19.** paper clip	de tres huecos	
calendario de escritorio	**7.** desk calendar	ganchos (para papeles)	dispenser	tampón/almohadilla de	**30.** stamp pad/ink pad
lámpara	**8.** desk lamp	depresillas/portaganchos/		tinta	
placa	**9.** nameplate	portaclips/cajita		sello de goma	**31.** rubber stamp
carpeta (para el	**10.** desk pad	para ganchos		pluma estilográfica/	**32.** pen
escritorio)/de felpa		tarjetas personales	**20.** business cards	pluma/estilográfica	
papelero/cesto/canasta	**11.** wastebasket	sujetapapel/tabla/tablilla	**21.** clipboard	lápiz	**33.** pencil
para papeles		agenda	**22.** appointment book	bolígrafo	**34.** mechanical pencil
silla de secretaria	**12.** posture chair/	agenda personal	**23.** organizer/	marcador	**35.** highlighter (pen)
	clerical chair		personal planner	borrador	**36.** eraser
calendario de pared	**13.** wall calendar	hoja de asistencia	**24.** timesheet		

[1–15]
A. Welcome to the company.
B. Thank you.
A. How do you like your _____?
B. It's/They're very nice.

[16–36]
A. My desk is such a mess! I can't find my _____!
B. Here it is/Here they are next to your _____.

Which items on this page do you have? Do you have an appointment book, personal planner, or calendar? How do you remember important things such as appointments, meetings, and birthdays?

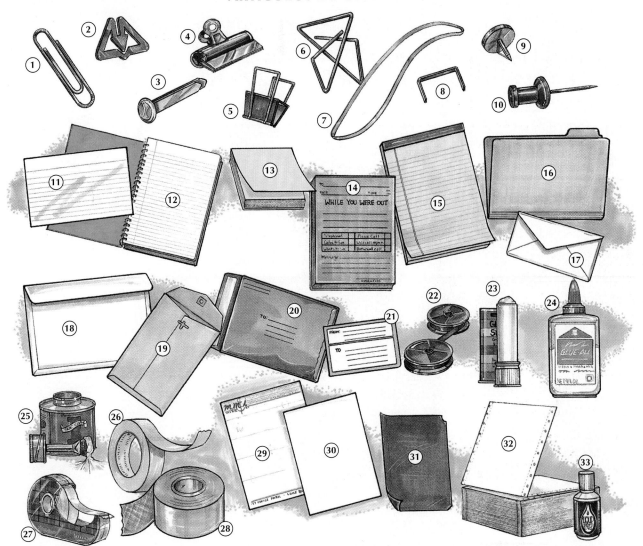

sujetapapeles/gancho	**1.** paper clip	libretita de notas autoadhesivas	**13.** Post-It note pad	goma/pegamento	**24.** glue
sujetapapeles/gancho plástico para papeles	**2.** plastic clip	libreta/papeles para mensajes	**14.** message pad	pegalotodo/goma sintética	**25.** rubber cement
sujetapapeles	**3.** paper fastener	libreta/papeles tamaño legal	**15.** legal pad	cinta adhesiva	**26.** masking tape
sujetapapeles/ gancho chato para papeles	**4.** bulldog clip	carpeta/archivo	**16.** file folder/ manila folder	cinta pegante/ adhesiva	**27.** Scotch tape/ cellophane tape
sujetapapeles para carpetas	**5.** binder clip	sobre	**17.** envelope	cinta pegante de celofán	**28.** sealing tape/ package mailing tape
sujetapapeles/mariposa	**6.** clamp	sobre acolchado	**18.** catalog envelope	papel para escribir cartas	**29.** stationery
liga/goma	**7.** rubber band	sobre de papel manila	**19.** clasp envelope	papel para escribir a máquina	**30.** typing paper
grapa	**8.** staple	sobre para correo aéreo	**20.** mailer	papel carbón	**31.** carbon paper
tachuela	**9.** thumbtack	etiqueta	**21.** mailing label	papel para computadoras	**32.** computer paper
chicheta	**10.** pushpin	cinta (para máquina de escribir)	**22.** typewriter ribbon	líquido corrector	**33.** correction fluid
ficha	**11.** index card	goma en barra	**23.** gluestick		
libreta de notas	**12.** memo pad/ note pad				

A. { We've run out of __[1–23]__ s.
{ We've run out of __[24–33]__ .

B. I'll get some more from the supply room.

A. Could I borrow a/an/some __[1–33]__ ?

B. Sure. Here you are.

reloj marcador	**1.** time clock	capataz	**10.** foreman	máquina dispensadora/	**19.** vending machine
tarjetas (de asistencia)	**2.** time cards	máquina	**11.** machine	vendedora automática	
cuarto de suministros	**3.** supply room	palanca	**12.** lever	circular del sindicato	**20.** union notice
anteojos/lentes protectores/	**4.** safety glasses	extinguidor de fuego/	**13.** fire extinguisher	buzón de sugerencias	**21.** suggestion box
gafas protectoras		extintor		cafetería	**22.** cafeteria
máscaras	**5.** masks	maletín de primeros auxilios	**14.** first-aid kit	sección de envíos	**23.** shipping
cadena/línea de montaje	**6.** (assembly) line	cinta/correa	**15.** conveyor belt		department
obrero/operario	**7.** worker	transportadora		carrito manual	**24.** hand truck
lugar/posición de trabajo	**8.** work station	almacén/depósito	**16.** warehouse	muelle de carga	**25.** loading dock
supervisor	**9.** quality control	portacarga	**17.** forklift	oficina de pagos	**26.** payroll office
	supervisor	montacarga	**18.** freight elevator	oficina de personal	**27.** personnel office

A. Excuse me. I'm a new employee.
Where's/Where are the _____?
B. Next to/Near/In/On the _____.

A. Have you seen *Fred*?
B. Yes. He's in/on/at/next to/near
the _____.

Are there any factories where you live? What kind?
What are the working conditions there?

What products do factories in your country produce?

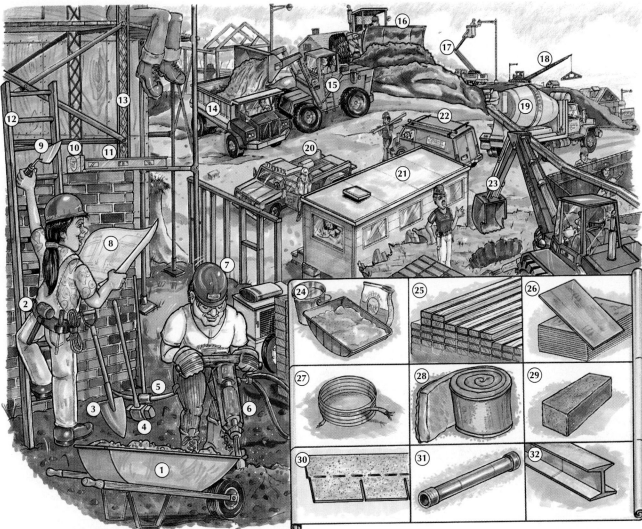

carretilla	**1.** wheelbarrow
cinturón para herramientas	**2.** toolbelt
pala	**3.** shovel
almádena/mazo(a)	**4.** sledgehammer
pico	**5.** pickax
martillo perforador/ neumático	**6.** jackhammer/ pneumatic drill
casco de construcción	**7.** helmet/hard hat
planos	**8.** blueprints
paleta de albañil/ palustre/palaustre	**9.** trowel
cinta métrica/ de medir	**10.** tape measure
nivel /nivel de aire/ nivel de burbuja	**11.** level

escalera	**12.** ladder
andamio	**13.** scaffolding
volquete/camión de volquete/de volteo	**14.** dump truck
cargadora/ pala cargadora	**15.** front-end loader
excavadora/pala excavadora/buldozer	**16.** bulldozer
grúa (con plataforma movible)	**17.** cherry picker
grúa	**18.** crane
hormigonera/concretera/ mezcladora de cemento	**19.** cement mixer
camión de carga/ camión de reparto	**20.** pickup truck
casa remolque/ casa rodante	**21.** trailer

vagón de carga/ furgoneta/troca	**22.** van
tractor excavador/ pala excavadora	**23.** backhoe
cemento	**24.** cement
madera	**25.** wood/lumber
madera contrachapeada/ madera prensada	**26.** plywood
alambre	**27.** wire
fibra aisladora	**28.** insulation
ladrillo	**29.** brick
teja	**30.** shingle
tubería/tubo/pipa/paipa	**31.** pipe
viga	**32.** girder/beam

[1–12]
A. Could you get me that/those _____?
B. Sure.

[13–23]
A. Watch out for that _____!
B. Oh! Thanks for the warning!

[24–32]
A. Are we going to have enough _[24–28]_ / _[29–32]_ s to finish the job?
B. I think so.

EL AUTOMÓVIL/EL COCHE/EL CARRO

luces delanteras/faros	**1.** headlight	rejilla/parrilla portaequipaje/baca	**13.** luggage rack/ luggage carrier	bujías	**30.** spark plugs
parachoques/defensa	**2.** bumper	parabrisas trasero	**14.** rear windshield	carburador	**31.** carburetor
luz direccional/luz intermitente	**3.** turn signal	descongelador/ desempañador/	**15.** rear defroster	filtro	**32.** air filter
señal de estacionamiento/luz de aparcamiento/ de posición	**4.** parking light	de vidrio trasero maletero/baúl/cajuela	**16.** trunk	batería indicador de aceite/ varilla del aceite	**33.** battery **34.** dipstick
llanta/neumático/ goma	**5.** tire	luz (trasera) luz del freno/	**17.** taillight **18.** brake light	alternador radiador	**35.** alternator **36.** radiator
tapacubos/embelle- cedor/pollera/copa	**6.** hubcap	indicadora de frenado luz de retroceso	**19.** backup light	banda/correa del ventilador	**37.** fan belt
toldo/capota/ capó del motor	**7.** hood	placa/chapa de matrícula/ tablilla	**20.** license plate	manguera/ manga del radiador	**38.** radiator hose
parabrisas/cristal delantero	**8.** windshield	tubo de escape	**21.** tailpipe	gasolinera/bomba/ estación de gasolina	**39.** gas station/ service station
limpiaparabrisas/ cepillo	**9.** windshield wipers	silenciador transmisión	**22.** muffler **23.** transmission	bomba de aire crujía/zona/área	**40.** air pump **41.** service bay
espejo lateral/espejo retrovisor exterior	**10.** side mirror	tanque (de gasolina) gato	**24.** gas tank **25.** jack	de servicio mecánico(a)	**42.** mechanic
antena	**11.** antenna	llanta de repuesto	**26.** spare tire	ayudante/asistente	**43.** attendant
media luna/ quemacoco/	**12.** sunroof	señales de peligro/ señales de bengala	**27.** flare	surtidor/bomba/ pompa de gasolina	**44.** gas pump
tragaluz/claraboya		cables de conexión/ reactivadores	**28.** jumper cables	boca/boquilla	**45.** nozzle
		motor	**29.** engine		

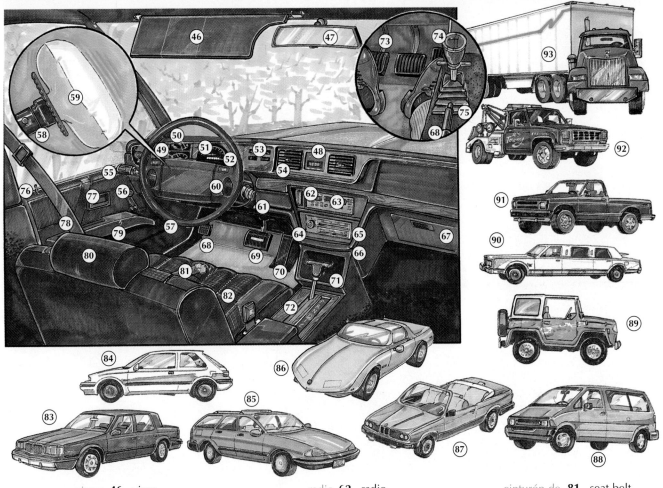

visera	**46.** visor
espejo retrovisor	**47.** rearview mirror
tablero/panel de instru-	**48.** dashboard/
mentos/de mandos	instrument panel
medidor/	**49.** gas gauge/
indicador de gasolina	fuel gauge
medidora/indicador	**50.** temperature gauge
de temperatura	
velocímetro	**51.** speedometer
odómetro	**52.** odometer
señal de alarma/luz	**53.** warning lights
(indicadora) de alarma	
ventilador	**54.** vent
palanca de	**55.** turn signal
direccionales	
piloto/control de	**56.** cruise control
travesía/control de	
velocidad automático	
volante/guía/timón	**57.** steering wheel
eje	**58.** steering column
bolsa de aire	**59.** air bag
claxón/bocina/pito	**60.** horn
encendido	**61.** ignition

radio	**62.** radio
casetera	**63.** tape/cassette player
aire acondicionado	**64.** air conditioning
calefacción	**65.** heater
descongelador/	**66.** defroster
desempañador	
guantera/gaveta	**67.** glove compartment
freno de emergencia	**68.** emergency brake
freno	**69.** brake
acelerador	**70.** accelerator/gas pedal
engranaje de cambios	**71.** gearshift
mando de transmisión	**72.** automatic
automática	transmission
embrague/clutch	**73.** clutch
palanca/mando	**74.** stickshift
de cambios	
transmisión manual	**75.** manual transmission
seguro	**76.** door lock
manija/manilla/	**77.** door handle
manigueta	
cinturón de seguridad	**78.** shoulder harness
brazo	**79.** armrest
cabezal/protector de cabeza	**80.** headrest

cinturón de	**81.** seat belt
seguridad	
asiento	**82.** seat
sedán	**83.** sedan
cupé/carro	**84.** hatchback
de tres puertas	
camioneta/	**85.** station wagon
ranchera/vagoneta	
carro/coche	**86.** sports car
deportivo	
convertible/	**87.** convertible
descapotable	
microbús/busito/	**88.** minivan
minibús	
todoterreno/jeep	**89.** jeep
limusina	**90.** limousine
camioneta/	**91.** pick-up truck
furgoneta	
de repartos/pick-up	
camión remolque/	**92.** tow truck
grúa	
camión/troca	**93.** truck

[1, 3, 8–15, 23, 34–38, 46–82]
A. What's the matter with your car?
B. The _____(s) is/are broken.

[1, 4–6, 9–11, 30–33, 37, 38]
A. Can I help you?
B. Yes. I need to replace a/the _____(s).

[1, 2, 4–8, 10–14, 16–20]
A. I was just in a car accident!
B. Oh, no! Were you hurt?
A. No. But my _____(s) was/were damaged.

túnel	**1.** tunnel	isla/jardín	**13.** median	área de servicios	**24.** service area

túnel **1.** tunnel
puente **2.** bridge
caseta/cabina/garita **3.** tollbooth
de peaje
fila de importe/ **4.** exact change lane
cambio exacto
letrero/ **5.** route sign
indicador de rutas
autopista **6.** highway
carretera **7.** road
muro/divisor/ **8.** divider/barrier
división central
paso elevado/puente **9.** overpass
paso bajo el elevado **10.** underpass
carril de entrada/ **11.** entrance ramp/
rampa de entrada on ramp
autopista interestatal **12.** interstate (highway)

isla/jardín **13.** median
divisor/vereda/camellón
carril izquierdo **14.** left lane
carril central **15.** middle lane/
center lane
carril derecho **16.** right lane
hombro/borde/ **17.** shoulder
orilla de la carretera
línea discontinua de "se **18.** broken line
puede pasar"
línea de "no pase"/ **19.** solid line
línea de "no pasar"
letrero de límite **20.** speed limit sign
de velocidad
carril/rampa de salida **21.** exit (ramp)
letrero de salida **22.** exit sign
letrero de **23.** yield sign
"ceda el paso"

área de servicios **24.** service area
cruce (del tren) **25.** railroad crossing
calle **26.** street
calle de una vía **27.** one-way street
línea amarilla doble **28.** double yellow line
de "no doble"/de "no doblar"
vía peatonal/paso peatonal/ **29.** crosswalk
cruce de peatones/línea de
seguridad
cruce **30.** intersection
cruce escolar **31.** school crossing
esquina **32.** corner
semáforo **33.** traffic light/signal
señal de "no gire/ **34.** no left turn sign
doble a la izquierda"
señal de "no gire/ **35.** no right turn sign
doble a la derecha"
señal de "no gire/ **36.** no U-turn sign
doble en U"
señal de "no entre" **37.** do not enter sign
señal de "alto" **38.** stop sign

A. Where's the
accident?
B. It's on/in/at/near
the _____.

Describe a highway you travel on.
Describe an intersection near where you live.

In your area, on which highways and streets do most
accidents occur? Why are these places dangerous?

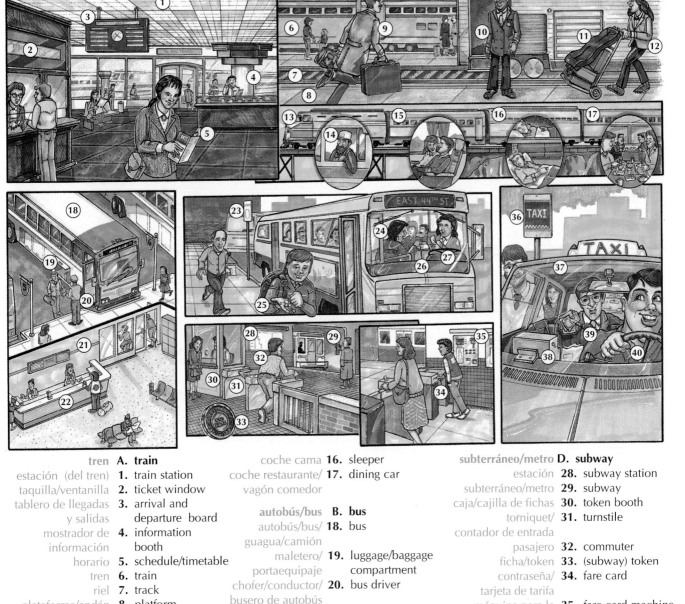

tren	**A. train**
estación (del tren)	**1.** train station
taquilla/ventanilla	**2.** ticket window
tablero de llegadas y salidas	**3.** arrival and departure board
mostrador de información	**4.** information booth
horario	**5.** schedule/timetable
tren	**6.** train
riel	**7.** track
plataforma/andén	**8.** platform
pasajero	**9.** passenger
cobrador(a)/ inspector(a)	**10.** conductor
equipaje	**11.** luggage/baggage
maletero(a)	**12.** porter/redcap
locomotora	**13.** engine
maquinista/ conductor(a)	**14.** engineer
vagón/coche de pasajeros	**15.** passenger car

coche cama	**16.** sleeper
coche restaurante/ vagón comedor	**17.** dining car

autobús/bus	**B. bus**
autobús/bus/ guagua/camión	**18.** bus
maletero/ portaequipaje	**19.** luggage/baggage compartment
chofer/conductor/ busero de autobús	**20.** bus driver
estación de autobuses	**21.** bus station
mostrador de venta de boletos/boletería	**22.** ticket counter

autobús/bus	**C. local bus**
parada/paradero de autobuses	**23.** bus stop
pasajero	**24.** rider/passenger
tarifa	**25.** (bus) fare
caja/cajilla de tarifas	**26.** fare box
trasbordo	**27.** transfer

subterráneo/metro	**D. subway**
estación	**28.** subway station
subterráneo/metro	**29.** subway
caja/cajilla de fichas	**30.** token booth
torniquet/ contador de entrada	**31.** turnstile
pasajero	**32.** commuter
ficha/token	**33.** (subway) token
contraseña/ tarjeta de tarifa	**34.** fare card
máquina para la contraseña/para la tarifa	**35.** fare card machine

taxi	**E. taxi**
parada de taxis/ piquera	**36.** taxi stand
taxi	**37.** taxi/cab/taxicab
medidor/marcador	**38.** meter
tarifa	**39.** fare
taxista/chofer de taxi	**40.** cab driver/taxi driver

[A–E]
A. How are you going to get there?
B. { I'm going to take the [A–D] .
   { I'm going to take a [E] .

[1–8, 10–23, 26, 28–31, 35, 36]
A. Excuse me. Where's the _____?
B. Over there.

EL AEROPUERTO

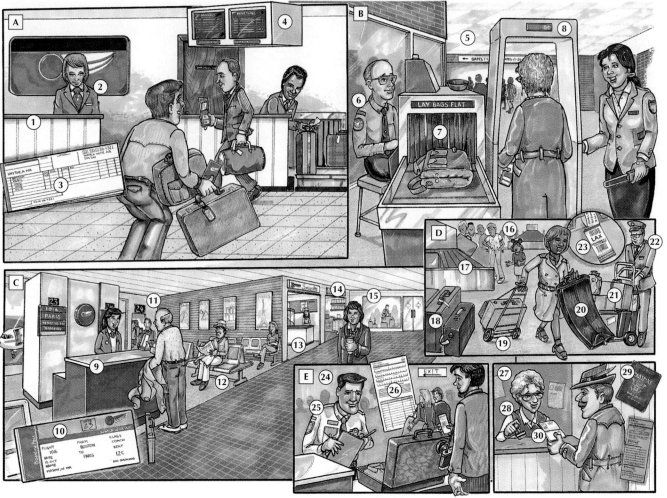

Registro/Chequeo (de pasajeros)	A. Check-In
mostrador de pasajes	1. ticket counter
expendedor de pasajes	2. ticket agent
pasaje/boleto/billete	3. ticket
monitor de llegadas y salidas	4. arrival and departure monitor

Seguridad	B. Security
control/puesto de seguridad	5. security checkpoint
guarda/guardia de seguridad	6. security guard
máquina de rayos x (equis)	7. X-ray machine
detector de metales	8. metal detector

El area/La sala de entradas y salidas	C. The Gate
mostrador de factura/registro/chequeo	9. check-in counter
pase de abordaje	10. boarding pass
puerta/sala	11. gate
sala de espera	12. waiting area
kiosko/puesto de refrescos/	13. concession stand/snack bar
de comida/de botanas	
tienda	14. gift shop
almacén/tienda libre de impuestos	15. duty-free shop

Reclamo/Retiro de equipaje	D. Baggage Claim
área de reclamo/	16. baggage claim (area)
de retiro de equipaje	
banda/carrusel/	17. baggage carousel
rodocarga de equipaje	
maleta	18. suitcase
carrito para maletas/portaequipaje	19. luggage carrier
bolsa para trajes/vestidos/	20. garment bag
sacos y abrigos	
equipaje	21. baggage
mozo/portero	22. porter/skycap
etiqueta/boleto de factura del equipaje	23. (baggage) claim check

Emigración y Aduana	E. Customs and Immigration
aduana	24. customs
empleado/oficial de aduana	25. customs officer
tarjeta/forma de declaración	26. customs declaration form
de aduana	
emigración/inmigración	27. immigration
empleado de emigración/inmigración	28. immigration officer
pasaporte	29. passport
visa	30. visa

[1, 2, 4–9, 11–17, 24, 25, 27, 28]
A. Excuse me. Where's the _____?*
B. Right over there.

*With 24 and 27, use: Excuse me. Where's _____?

[3, 10, 18–21, 23, 26, 29, 30]
A. Oh, no! I think I've lost my _____!
B. I'll help you look for it.

EL AVIÓN

cabina (de mando)	**1.** cockpit	cinturón de seguridad	**15.** seat belt	bolsa para mareos	**30.** air sickness bag
piloto	**2.** pilot/captain	asiento de ventanilla	**16.** window seat	chaleco salvavidas	**31.** life vest
copiloto	**3.** co-pilot	asiento central	**17.** middle seat	pista	**32.** runway
panel/tablero de	**4.** instrument	asiento de pasillo	**18.** aisle seat	terminal (edificio)	**33.** terminal (building)
instrumentos	panel	señal de "abrócharse	**19.** Fasten Seat Belt	torre de control	**34.** control tower
ingeniero de vuelo	**5.** flight engineer	los cinturones"	sign	aeroplano/avión de	**35.** airplane/plane/jet
sección de primera	**6.** first-class section	señal de "no fumar"	**20.** No Smoking sign	propulsión a chorro/jet	
clase		mando/botón de	**21.** call button	nariz (del avión)	**36.** nose
pasajero	**7.** passenger	llamada/de servicio		fuselaje	**37.** fuselage
pasillo de abordaje	**8.** galley	mascarilla de oxígeno	**22.** oxygen mask	puerta de carga/	**38.** cargo door
aeromoza/azafata/	**9.** flight attendant	puerta de emergencia	**23.** emergency exit	de la bodega	
el sobrecargo/		brazo	**24.** armrest	tren de aterrizaje	**39.** landing gear
la sobrecargo		mando/botone de	**25.** seat control	ala	**40.** wing
baño	**10.** lavatory/bathroom	control/del asiento		turbina	**41.** engine
cabina	**11.** cabin	mesa	**26.** tray (table)	cola	**42.** tail
equipaje de mano	**12.** carry-on bag	comida	**27.** meal	avión de hélice	**43.** propeller plane/prop
compartimiento	**13.** overhead	bosillo del asiento	**28.** seat pocket	hélice	**44.** propeller
superior	compartment	tarjeta de instrucciones	**29.** emergency instrution	helicóptero	**45.** helicopter
pasillo	**14.** aisle	de emergencia	card	rotor del helicóptero	**46.** rotor (blade)

A. Where's the _____?
B. In/On/Next to/Behind/In front of/Above/
   Below the _____.

Ladies and gentlemen. This is your captain
speaking. I'm sorry for the delay. We had a little
problem with one of our _____s.* Everything
is fine now and we'll be taking off shortly.

*Use 4, 7, 10, 12, 20–22, 24.

Estado del tiempo	A. Weather				
soleado	1. sunny	granizando	11. hailing	caliente	21. hot
nublado	2. cloudy	callisqueando/helando	12. sleeting	caluroso/cálido	22. warm
despejado	3. clear	relámpago(s)/	13. lightning	fresco	23. cool
brumoso/con bruma/	4. hazy	relampagueando		frío	24. cold
con calina		tormenta de truenos	14. thunderstorm	helado	25. freezing
con niebla/con neblina	5. foggy	tormenta de nieve	15. snowstorm		
con viento/ventoso	6. windy	huracán/tifón	16. hurricane/typhoon	**Estaciones**	**C. Seasons**
húmedo/	7. humid/	tornado/torbellino	17. tornado	verano	26. summer
pegajoso/bochornoso	muggy			otoño	27. fall/autumn
lloviendo	8. raining	**Temperatura ambiental**	**B. Temperature**	invierno	28. winter
lloviznando	9. drizzling	termómetro	18. thermometer	primavera	29. spring
nevando	10. snowing	Farenheit	19. Fahrenheit		
		Centígrado/Celcius	20. Centigrade/Celsius		

[1–12]
A. What's the weather like?
B. It's _____.

[13–17]
A. What's the weather forecast?
B. There's going to be
    _[13]_ /a _[14–17]_ .

[19–25]
A. How's the weather?
B. It's _[21–25]_ .
A. What's the temperature?
B. It's ……. degrees _[19, 20]_ .

Describe the seasons where you live.
Tell about the weather and the temperature.

What's your favorite season?
Why?

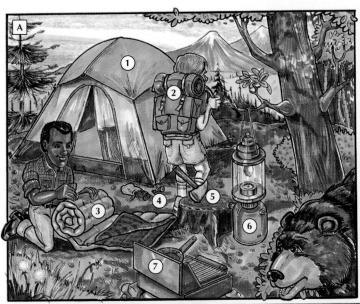

acampar	**A. camping**
tienda de campaña	**1.** tent
mochila	**2.** backpack
bolsa de dormir	**3.** sleeping bag
estacas	**4.** tent stakes
hacha	**5.** hatchet
lámpara de gas	**6.** lantern
hornilla	**7.** camp stove

ir de excursión (excursionismo)	**B. hiking**
botas para ir de excursión	**8.** hiking boots
brújula/compás	**9.** compass
mapa	**10.** trail map

hacer alpinismo/ montañismo/ escalar montañas	**C. mountain climbing**
botas para escalar	**11.** hiking boots

escalar rocas/ hacer escalada	**D. rock climbing**
cuerda (de nudos para trepar)	**12.** rope
aparejo	**13.** harness

merendar/comer al aire libre/ ir de picnic	**E. picnic**
manta	**14.** (picnic) blanket
termo	**15.** thermos
canasta/cesto	**16.** picnic basket

[A–E]

A. Let's go _____* this weekend.

B. Good idea! We haven't gone _____*
   in a long time.

*With E, say: on a picnic

[1–16]

A. Did you bring the _____?

B. Yes, I did.

Have you ever gone camping or hiking?
Where? What equipment did you use?

Do you like to go on picnics? Where?
What picnic supplies and food do you take with you?

pista/andador/andadero para trotar	**1.** jogging path	zoológico	**10.** zoo	pasamano **20.** monkey bars
baños públicos	**2.** rest rooms	fuente	**11.** water fountain	deslizadero/tobogán/ **21.** slide resbaladero/zurradero
estatua	**3.** statue	concha acústica	**12.** band shell	columpios **22.** swings
merendero/área para merendar/área de picnic	**4.** picnic area	camino para caballos/ de herradura	**13.** bridle path	columpio de llantas/de gomas **23.** tire swing
mesa para merendar/ para hacer picnic	**5.** picnic table	rejilla/soporte para bicicletas	**14.** bike rack	sube y baja/subibaja/ **24.** seesaw tintibajo/balancín
parrilla	**6.** grill	estanque para patos	**15.** duck pond	piscina infantil/ **25.** wading pool
basurero/zafacón	**7.** trash can	camino/cancha/pista para bicicletas	**16.** bicycle path/ bikeway	chapoteadero(a)/alberca/ pileta para niños
caballitos/carrusel	**8.** merry-go-round/ carousel	banco	**17.** bench	cajón/caja de arena/arenero **26.** sandbox
fuente de agua	**9.** fountain	parque infantil/ parquecito para niños	**18.** playground	arena **27.** sand
		laberinto	**19.** jungle gym	

[1–18] A. Excuse me. Does this park have (a) _____?
B. Yes. Right over there.

[19–27] A. { Be careful on the [19–24] !
{ Be careful in the [25–27] !
B. I will, Mom/Dad.

Describe a park and a playground you are familiar with.

salvavidas	**1.** lifeguard	sombrilla de playa/parasol	**14.** beach umbrella	manta/frisa	**24.** (beach) blanket
silla de salvavidas	**2.** lifeguard stand	silla de playa	**15.** (beach) chair	sombrero de paja/	**25.** sun hat
salvavidas/flotador	**3.** life preserver	toalla de playa	**16.** (beach) towel	playero	
puesto de refrescos	**4.** snack bar/	vestido/traje de baño/	**17.** bathing suit/	anteojos/lentes de sol/	**26.** sunglasses
	refreshment stand	bañador	swimsuit	lentes oscuros/gafas	
duna de arena	**5.** sand dune	gorra de baño	**18.** bathing cap	de sol/gafas oscuras	
piedra/roca/peña	**6.** rock	tabla/planeador	**19.** kickboard	bronceador/loción	**27.** suntan lotion/
nadador	**7.** swimmer	pequeño		bronceadora/	sunscreen
ola	**8.** wave	tabla/planeador de mar/	**20.** surfboard	loción protectora/	
surfista	**9.** surfer	tabla hawaiana		bloqueador solar	
vendedor	**10.** vendor	cometa/papalote/chiringa/	**21.** kite	cubito/cubo	**28.** pail/bucket
tomador de	**11.** sunbather	volantín/chichigua/		palita/pala	**29.** shovel
sol/playero/secano/		birlocha/güila		pelota/balón/	**30.** beach ball
bañista de sol		balsa/colchoneta/	**22.** raft/air mattress	bola de playa	
castillo de arena	**12.** sand castle	colchón de aire/flotador		hielera/	**31.** cooler
concha	**13.** seashell/shell	tubo/llanta/goma	**23.** tube	nevera de playa	

[1–13]
A. What a nice beach!
B. It is. Look at all the _____s!

[14–31]
A. Are you ready for the beach?
B. Almost. I just have to get my _____.

Do you like to go to the beach? Describe your favorite beach. What do you take when you go there?

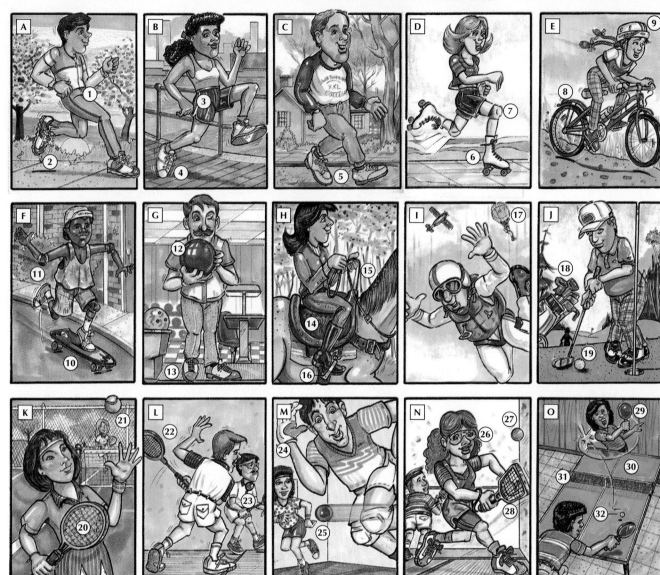

hacer footing/correr al trote/trotar/ ir de caminata	**A. jogging**	monopatinaje/ patinaje	**F. skateboarding**	(e)squash	**L. squash**
sudadero(a)/chándal	**1.** jogging suit	monopatín/patín/patineta	**10.** skateboard	raqueta de (e)squash	**22.** squash racquet
zapatos/zapatillas para correr/zapatillas para trotar/deportivas(os)	**2.** jogging shoes	codal /coderos/corderas	**11.** elbow pads	pelota/bola de (e)squash	**23.** squash ball
		boliche/bolos	**G. bowling**	frontón de mano/ pelota vasca/ jai a lai/handbol	**M. handball**
correr	**B. running**	bola (de boliche)	**12.** bowling ball	guante	**24.** handball glove
pantalonetas/ calzonas deportivas	**3.** running shorts	zapatos para jugar boliche	**13.** bowling shoes	pelota/bola	**25.** handball
zapatos/zapatillas para correr/tenis de correr	**4.** running shoes	equitación	**H. horseback riding**		
		silla de montar/montura	**14.** saddle	frontón con raqueta/ pelota vasca/racquetball	**N. racquetball**
caminar	**C. walking**	riendas	**15.** reins	lentes protectores de ojos/ gafas protectoras de ojos	**26.** safety goggles
zapatos/zapatillas para caminar	**5.** walking shoes	estribos	**16.** stirrups	pelota/bola de frontón	**27.** racquetball
		paracaidismo/ caída libre	**I. skydiving**	raqueta/canalete	**28.** racquet
patinar/patinaje	**D. roller skating**	paracaídas	**17.** parachute	pimpón/tenis de mesa/ ping-pong	**O. ping pong**
patines (de ruedas)	**6.** roller skates	golf	**J. golf**	raqueta/paleta	**29.** paddle
rodilleras	**7.** knee pads	palo de golf	**18.** golf clubs	mesa para jugar pimpón	**30.** ping pong table
		pelota/bola de golf	**19.** golf ball	malla/red	**31.** net
ciclismo	**E. cycling/bicycling/ biking**	tenis	**K. tennis**	pelota/bola de pimpón	**32.** ping pong ball
bicicleta	**8.** bicycle/bike	raqueta de tenis	**20.** tennis racquet		
casco protector/yelmo/ chichonera (para niños)	**9.** (bicycle) helmet	pelota/bola de tenis	**21.** tennis ball		

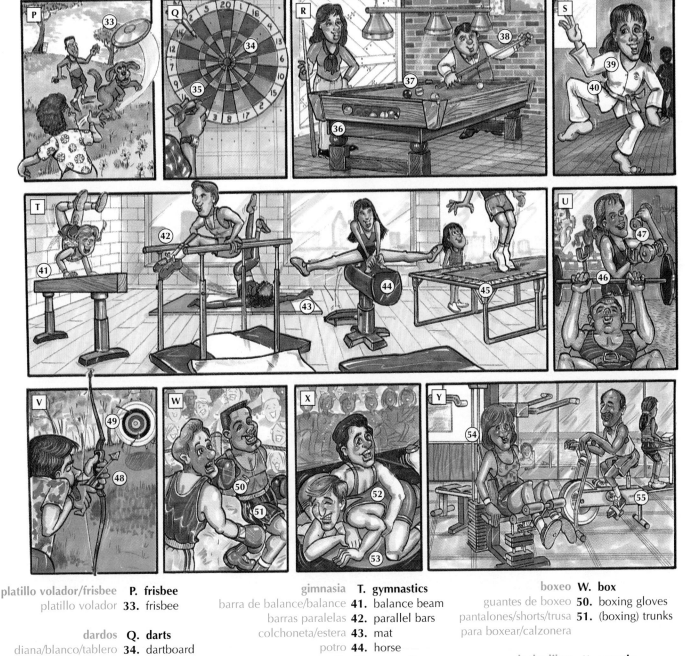

| platillo volador/frisbee | **P. frisbee** |
| platillo volador | **33.** frisbee |

dardos	**Q. darts**
diana/blanco/tablero	**34.** dartboard
para tiro al blanco	
dardos	**35.** darts

billar	**R. billiards/pool**
mesa de billar/chapolín	**36.** pool table
bolas de billar	**37.** billiard balls
taco/palo de billar	**38.** pool stick

karate	**S. karate**
uniforme de karate	**39.** karate outfit
cinturón/correa	**40.** karate belt

gimnasia	**T. gymnastics**
barra de balance/balance	**41.** balance beam
barras paralelas	**42.** parallel bars
colchoneta/estera	**43.** mat
potro	**44.** horse
trampolín	**45.** trampoline

levantamiento de pesas	**U. weightlifting**
barra con pesas	**46.** barbell
pesas/mancuernas	**47.** weights

arco	**V. archery**
arco y flecha	**48.** bow and arrow
diana/blanco	**49.** target

boxeo	**W. box**
guantes de boxeo	**50.** boxing gloves
pantalones/shorts/trusa	**51.** (boxing) trunks
para boxear/calzonera	

lucha libre	**X. wrestle**
uniforme	**52.** wrestling uniform
lona/estera/cuadrilátero	**53.** (wrestling) mat

ejercicio	**Y. work out**
equipo de ejercicios	**54.** universal/exercise
para estar en forma	equipment
bicicleta estacionaria/	**55.** exercise bike
bicicleta estática	

[A–Y]

A. What do you like to do in your free time?

B.
{ I like to go [A–I] .
I like to play [J–R] .
I like to do [S–V] .
I like to [W–Y] . }

[1–55]

A. I really like this/these new _____.

B. It's/They're very nice.

DEPORTES EN EQUIPO

[A–H]
A. Do you like **baseball**?
B. Yes. **Baseball** is one of my favorite sports.

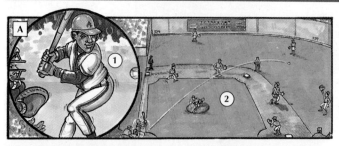

béisbol A. baseball
jugador de béisbol **1.** baseball player
campo de juego/ **2.** baseball field/
diamante de béisbol ballfield

softball/sófbol B. softball
jugador de sófbol **3.** softball player
campo de sófbol **4.** ballfield

fútbol americano C. football
jugador de fútbol **5.** football player
americano
campo de fútbol **6.** football field
americano

lacrosse/cross D. lacrosse
jugador de lacrosse/ **7.** lacrosse player
de cross
campo de lacrosse/ **8.** lacrosse field
de cross

hockey sobre hielo E. (ice) hockey
jugador de hockey **9.** hockey player
pista de hielo **10.** hockey rink

baloncesto/básquetbol F. basketball
jugador de baloncesto/ **11.** basketball
de básquetbol player

cancha de baloncesto/ **12.** basketball
de básquetbol/ court
pista de baloncesto/
de básquetbol

voleibol/balonvolea G. volleyball
jugador de voleibol **13.** volleyball player
cancha de voleibol **14.** volleyball court

fútbol /fútbol soccer H. soccer
futbolista/ **15.** soccer player
jugador de fútbol
campo de fútbol **16.** soccer field

A. .... plays [A–H] very well.
B. You're right. I think he's/she's one
of the best _____s* on the team.

*Use 1, 3, 5, 7, 9, 11, 13, 15.

A. Now, listen! I want all of you
to go out on that _____† and
play the best game of [A–H]
you've ever played!
B. All right, Coach!

†Use 2, 4, 6, 8, 10, 12, 14, 16.

Which sports on this page do you like
to play? Which do you like to
watch?
What are your favorite teams?
Name some famous players of these
sports.

[1–27]
A. I can't find my **baseball**!
B. Look in the *closet.**

*closet, basement, garage

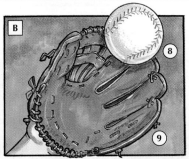

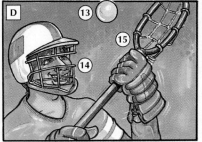

béisbol A. baseball
pelota de béisbol **1.** baseball
bate **2.** bat
casco de béisbol **3.** batting helmet
uniforme **4.** baseball uniform
máscara/protector **5.** catcher's mask
guante **6.** baseball glove
guante de receptor/ **7.** catcher's mitt
de catcher/
un mascota

softball/sófbol B. softball
pelota de softball/ **8.** softball
sófbol
guante **9.** softball glove

fútbol americano C. football
pelota de fútbol americano **10.** football
casco protector **11.** football helmet
protector de hombros(as) **12.** shoulder pads

lacrosse/cross D. lacrosse
pelota de lacrosse/de cross **13.** lacrosse ball
careta/máscara **14.** face guard
raqueta de lacrosse/ **15.** lacrosse stick
de cross

hockey sobre hielo E. hockey
disco **16.** hockey puck
palo/bastón de hockey **17.** hockey stick
máscara/careta **18.** hockey mask
guante de hockey **19.** hockey glove
patines de hockey **20.** hockey skates

baloncesto/básquetbol F. basketball
balón/pelota **21.** basketball
de baloncesto/
balón/pelota
de básquetbol
tablero **22.** backboard
canasta **23.** basketball hoop

voleibol/balonvolea G. volleyball
pelota/bola/de voleibo/ **24.** volleyball
pelota/bola/de volibol
red/malla **25.** volleyball net

fútbol/fútbol soccer/ H. soccer
balompié
balón de fútbol **26.** soccer ball
espinillera/polaina **27.** shinguards

[In a store]
A. Excuse me. I'm looking for
(a) [1–27].
B. All our [A–H] equipment is over
there.
A. Thanks.

[At home]
A. I'm going to play [A–H] after
school today.
B. Don't forget your [1–21, 24–27]!

Which sports on this page are popular
in your country? Which sports are
played in high school?

ACTIVIDADES Y DEPORTES DE INVIERNO

[A–H]
A. What's your favorite winter sport?
B. **Skiing**.

esquiar/hacer esquí alpino	**A. (downhill) skiing**	patinar sobre hielo	**C. (ice) skating**	hacer bobsleigh/	**F. bobsledding**
esquíes	**1.** skis	patines (de hielo)	**6.** (ice) skates	bambolear*me* sobre hielo	
botas de esquí/de esquiar	**2.** ski boots	protectores para	**7.** skate guards	bobsleigh/bobsled/	**11.** bobsled
ataduras/cogederas	**3.** bindings	patín de hielo		bob/bamboleador	
bastones/palos de esquí	**4.** poles				
		practicar patinaje artístico	**D. figure skating**	hacer travesía en	**G. snowmobiling**
hacer esquí nórdico/	**B. cross-country**	patines de hielo	**8.** figure skates	moto de nieve	
de fondo/esquiar	**skiing**			moto de nieve	**12.** snowmobile
a campo traviesa		deslizar*me* en	**E. sledding**		
esquíes	**5.** cross-country skis	trineo/en plato		descender en tobogán	**H. tobogganing**
		trineo	**9.** sled	tobogán	**13.** toboggan
		plato	**10.** sledding/dish/saucer		

[A–H]
[At work or at school on Friday]
A. What are you going to do this weekend?
B. I'm going to go _____.

[1–13]
[On the telephone]
A. Hello. Jimmy's Sporting Goods.
B. Hello. Do you sell _____(s)?
A. Yes, we do./No, we don't.

Have you ever watched the Winter Olympics? What is your favorite event? Which event do you think is the most exciting? the most dangerous?

[A–L]
A. Would you like to go **sailing** tomorrow?
B. Sure. I'd love to.

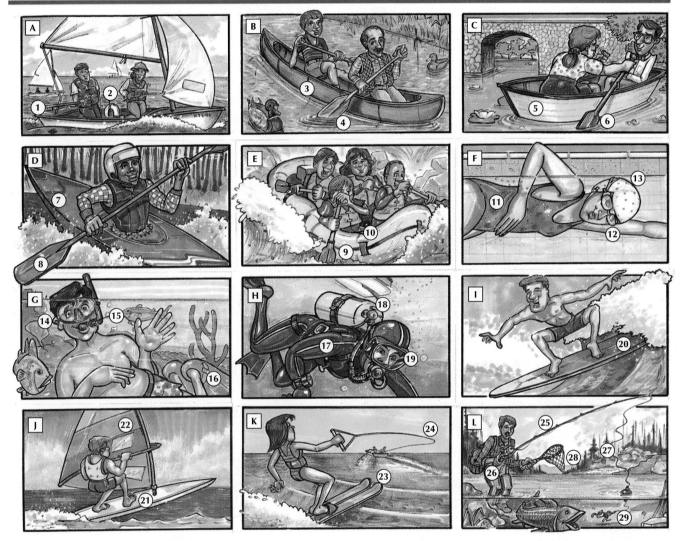

navegar en velero **A. sailing**	nadar **F. swimming**	surf/correr una ola **I. surfing**
velero/bote/ **1.** sailboat	vestido /traje de baño/ **11.** swimsuit/	tabla hawaiana/ **20.** surfboard
barco de vela	bañador	bathing suit	planeador de mar/
chaleco salvavidas/flotador **2.** life preserver	gafas de buceo **12.** goggles	tabla de surfing
	sin tanque/	
navegar en canoa (canotaje)/ **B. canoeing**	gafas saltonas	hacer plancha de vela/ **J. windsurfing**
piragüa (piragüismo)	gorra de baño **13.** bathing cap	correr una ola con tabla
canoa **3.** canoe		y vela/wind-surfing
pala/remo **4.** paddles	bucear sobre la **G. snorkeling**	tabla de vela **21.** sailboard
	superficie/bucear	vela **22.** sail
remar **C. rowing**	sin tanque/esnorquel	
bote de remos **5.** rowboat	visor/máscara **14.** mask	practicar esquí **K. waterskiing**
remos **6.** oars	tubo de **15.** snorkel	acuático
	respiración/esnorquel	esquíes (de agua) **23.** water skis
navegar en kayak **D. kayaking**	aletas/chapaletas **16.** flippers	cable/cuerda de **24.** towrope
kayak **7.** kayak		remolque
pala/remo **8.** paddle	bucear/hacer **H. scuba diving**	
	buceo submarino	pescar/ir de pesca **L. fishing**
descender en balsa **E. (white water)**	traje de buceo **17.** wet suit	caña de pescar **25.** (fishing) rod
rafting	tanque de aire **18.** (air) tank	carrete/bobina **26.** reel
balsa **9.** raft	máscara **19.** (diving) mask	sedal/cuerda **27.** (fishing) line
chaleco salvavidas **10.** life jacket		red **28.** net
		cebo/carnada **29.** bait

ACCIONES AL HACER DEPORTES Y EJERCICIOS

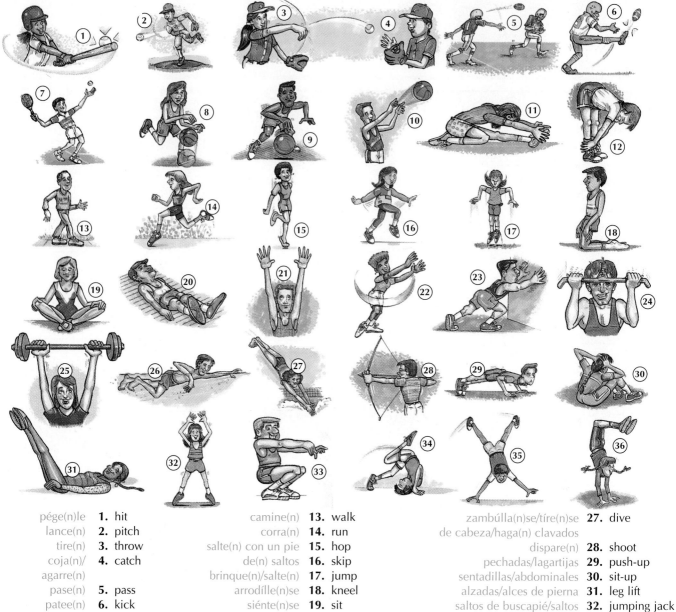

Spanish		English
pége(n)le	**1.**	hit
lance(n)	**2.**	pitch
tire(n)	**3.**	throw
coja(n)/	**4.**	catch
agarre(n)		
pase(n)	**5.**	pass
patee(n)	**6.**	kick
sirva(n)	**7.**	serve
rebote(n)	**8.**	bounce
drible(n)	**9.**	dribble
dispare(n)/	**10.**	shoot
tire(n)		
estíre(n)se	**11.**	stretch
dóble(n)se/	**12.**	bend
haga(n) flexiones		

Spanish		English
camine(n)	**13.**	walk
corra(n)	**14.**	run
salte(n) con un pie	**15.**	hop
de(n) saltos	**16.**	skip
brinque(n)/salte(n)	**17.**	jump
arrodílle(n)se	**18.**	kneel
siénte(n)se	**19.**	sit
acuéste(n)se	**20.**	lie down
estíre(n)se	**21.**	reach
balancée(n)se	**22.**	swing
empuje(n)	**23.**	push
hale(n)	**24.**	pull
levante(n)	**25.**	lift
nade(n)	**26.**	swim

Spanish		English
zambúlla(n)se/tíre(n)se de cabeza/haga(n) clavados	**27.**	dive
dispare(n)	**28.**	shoot
pechadas/lagartijas	**29.**	push-up
sentadillas/abdominales	**30.**	sit-up
alzadas/alces de pierna	**31.**	leg lift
saltos de buscapié/saltos con piernas y brazos separados	**32.**	jumping jack
dobleces de rodillas a fondo	**33.**	deep knee bend
volteretas	**34.**	somersault
medialunas/volteretas laterales	**35.**	cartwheel
hechuras de pino/posturas verticales apoyándose en las manos	**36.**	handstand

[1–10] A. _____ the ball!
      B. Okay, Coach!

[11–28] A. Now _____!
      B. Like this?
      A. Yes.

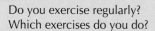

[29–36] A. Okay, everybody. I want you to do twenty _____s!
      B. Twenty _____s?!
      A. That's right.

Do you exercise regularly?
Which exercises do you do?

Be an exercise instructor. Lead your friends in an exercise routine using the actions on this page.

[A–Q]
A. What's your hobby?
B. **Sewing.**

coser	**A. sewing**	**pintar**	**H. painting**
máquina de coser	1. sewing machine	pincel	12. paintbrush
alfiler	2. pin	caballete	13. easel
alfiletero	3. pin cushion	pintura	14. paint
hilo	4. thread	**esculpir/escultura**	**I. sculpting/sculpture**
aguja de coser	5. (sewing) needle	yeso	15. plaster
dedal	6. thimble	piedra	16. stone
tela	7. material	**alfarería/cerámica**	**J. pottery**
tejer/hacer	**B. knitting**	arcilla	17. clay
tejido de punto		torno (de alfarero)	18. potter's wheel
aguja de tejer	8. knitting needle	**tallar en madera**	**K. woodworking**
hilo/lana para tejer	9. yarn	**coleccionar**	**L. stamp collecting**
hilar	**C. weaving**	**estampillas/sellos**	
rueca/telar	10. loom	álbum de estampillas/	19. stamp album
tejer/tejer a gancho	**D. crocheting**	de sellos	
gancho de tejer/	11. crochet hook	**coleccionar monedas**	**M. coin collecting**
aguja de gancho		catálogo de monedas	20. coin catalog
hacer tejido	**E. needlepoint**	álbum de monedas	21. coin album
en punto de cruz		**armar modelos**	**N. model building**
bordar	**F. embroidery**	modelo	22. model kit
acolchar/hacer colchas	**G. quilting**		

goma para armar modelos/	23. (model) glue
pegamento/pega	
pintura para modelos	24. (model) paint
observar/	**O. bird watching**
contemplar pájaros	
binoculares	25. binoculars
guía de terreno	26. field guide
fotografía	**P. photography**
cámara	27. camera
astronomía	**Q. astronomy**
telescopio	28. telescope
juegos	**R. games**
ajedrez	29. chess
damas/tablero	30. checkers
chaquete/tablas reales/negritas	31. backgammon
monopolio	32. Monopoly
rompecabezas/sopa de letras	33. Scrabble
barajas/naipes	34. cards
Trivia/Trivial Pursuit	35. Trivial Pursuit
canicas/bolas/bolitas	36. marbles
tabas/matatena/jacks	37. jacks

[1–28]   [In a store]
  A. May I help you?
  B. Yes, please. I'd like to buy
     (a/an) _____.

[29–37]   [At home]
  A. What do you want to do?
  B. Let's play _____.

What's your hobby?
What games are popular in your
  country? Describe how to play one.

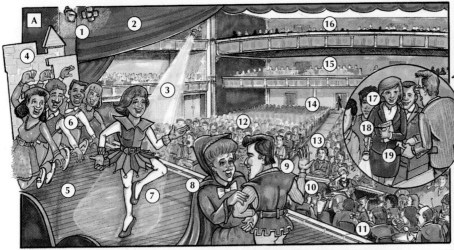

teatro	**A. theater**	luneta/platea	**14.** orchestra		ballet	**D. ballet**
luces	**1.** lights/lighting	entresuelo/entrepiso	**15.** mezzanine	bailarín	**27.** ballet dancer
telón	**2.** curtain	balcón/gallinero	**16.** balcony	bailarina/bailarina de ballet	**28.** ballerina
la perseguidora/reflector	**3.** spotlight	acomodador/guía	**17.** usher	compañía de ballet	**29.** ballet company
decorado/decorado	**4.** scenery	programa	**18.** program	zapatillas de ballet	**30.** ballet slippers
telón de fondo/ decoración		boleto/billete/tiquete	**19.** ticket	zapatillas de punta	**31.** toeshoes
escenario	**5.** stage	sinfónica	**B. symphony**	cine	**E. movies**
coro	**6.** chorus	orquesta sinfónica	**20.** symphony orchestra	marquesina/	**32.** marquee
bailarín, bailarina	**7.** dancer	músico	**21.** musician	portada de	
actriz	**8.** actress	director de orquesta	**22.** conductor	cine/cartelera	
actor	**9.** actor	batuta	**23.** baton	taquilla	**33.** box office
orquesta	**10.** orchestra	podio/tarima	**24.** podium	cartelera/cartel/valla	**34.** billboard
foso	**11.** orchestra pit	ópera	**C. opera**	publicitaria	
público	**12.** audience	cantante de ópera	**25.** opera singer	vestíbulo	**35.** lobby
pasillo	**13.** aisle	compañía de ópera	**26.** opera company	refresquería	**36.** refreshment stand
				pantalla	**37.** (movie) screen

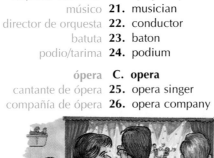

[A–E]
A. What are you doing this evening?
B. I'm going to the _____.

[1–11, 20–37]
A. { What a magnificent _____!
    { What magnificent _____s!
B. I agree.

[14–16]
A. Where did you sit during the performance?
B. We sat in the _____.

What kinds of entertainment on this page are popular in your country?

Tell about a play, concert, opera, ballet, or movie you have seen. Describe the performance and the theater.

TIPOS DE DIVERSIONES

música	**A. music**	obras de teatro	**B. plays**	programas de televisión	**D. TV programs**
música clásica	**1.** classical music	drama	**13.** drama	drama	**24.** drama
música popular	**2.** popular music	comedia	**14.** comedy	comedia	**25.** (situation) comedy/
música country/música	**3.** country music	comedia musical	**15.** musical (comedy)		sitcom
regional norteamericana				programa periodístico/	**26.** talk show
música rock	**4.** rock music	cine	**C. movies**	de opiniones	
música folklórica	**5.** folk music	drama	**16.** drama	programa de juegos	**27.** game show
música rap	**6.** rap music	comedia	**17.** comedy	noticiero/telediario	**28.** news program
gospel/música	**7.** gospel music	película del oeste	**18.** western	teledeportes	**29.** sports program
religiosa evangélica		cómicas/dibujos	**19.** cartoon	programa infantil	**30.** children's program
		animados/caricaturas		cómicas/caricaturas	**31.** cartoon
jazz	**8.** jazz	película extranjera	**20.** foreign film		
blues	**9.** blues	película de aventuras	**21.** adventure movie		
bluegrass	**10.** bluegrass	película de guerra	**22.** war movie		
rock ácido	**11.** heavy metal	película de	**23.** science fiction movie		
regae	**12.** reggae	ciencia ficción			

A. What kind of [A–D] do you like?

B. { I like [1–12] .
  { I like [13–31] s.

What's your favorite type of music?
Who is your favorite singer? musician?
   musical group?

What kind of movies do you like?
Who are your favorite movie stars?
What are the titles of your favorite
   movies?

What kind of TV programs do you like?
What are your favorite shows?

INSTRUMENTOS MUSICALES

A. Do you play a musical instrument?
B. Yes. I play the **violin**.

Instrumentos de cuerda	**A. Strings**
violín	**1.** violin
viola	**2.** viola
violoncello/cello	**3.** cello
bajo/contrabajo/violón	**4.** bass
guitarra (acústica)	**5.** (acoustic) guitar
ukelele	**6.** ukelele
guitarra eléctrica	**7.** electric guitar
banjo	**8.** banjo
mandolina	**9.** mandolin
arpa	**10.** harp

Instrumentos de viento	**B. Woodwinds**
pícolo/flautín	**11.** piccolo
flauta	**12.** flute
clarinete	**13.** clarinet
oboe	**14.** oboe
flauta dulce	**15.** recorder
saxofón	**16.** saxophone
fagot	**17.** bassoon

Instrumentos de metales	**C. Brass**
trompeta	**18.** trumpet
trombón	**19.** trombone
corno francés/trompa	**20.** French horn
tuba	**21.** tuba

Instrumentos de percusión	**D. Percussion**
tambor	**22.** drum
timbal	**23.** kettle drum
bongos	**24.** bongos
conga	**25.** conga (drum)

platillos	**26.** cymbals
xilófono	**27.** xylophone

Instrumentos de teclado	**E. Keyboard Instruments**
piano	**28.** piano
órgano	**29.** organ
piano eléctrico	**30.** electric piano/digital piano
organo con sintetizador	**31.** synthesizer

Otros instrumentos	**F. Other Instruments**
acordeón	**32.** accordion
harmónica	**33.** harmonica

A. You play the _____ very well.
B. Thank you.

A. What's that noise?
B. That's my son/daughter practicing the _____.

Do you play a musical instrument? Which one?
Name and describe other musical instruments used in your country.

árbol	**1.** tree	roble	**19.** oak	pensamiento	**36.** pansy
hoja–hojas	**2.** leaf–leaves	pino	**20.** pine	petunia	**37.** petunia
ramita/bejuco	**3.** twig	secoya	**21.** redwood	orquídea	**38.** orchid
rama	**4.** branch	sauce llorón	**22.** (weeping) willow	rosa	**39.** rose
brazo	**5.** limb	flor	**23.** flower	girasol	**40.** sunflower
tronco	**6.** trunk	pétalo	**24.** petal	tulipán	**41.** tulip
corteza	**7.** bark	pistilo	**25.** pistula	violeta	**42.** violet
raíz	**8.** root	estambre	**26.** stamen	arbusto	**43.** bush
aguja	**9.** needle	tallo	**27.** stem	arbusto (podado)	**44.** shrub
cono	**10.** cone	botón/capullo	**28.** bud	helecho	**45.** fern
cornejo	**11.** dogwood	espina	**29.** thorn	mata/planta	**46.** plant
acebo	**12.** holly	bulbo/cebolleta	**30.** bulb	cactus	**47.** cactus–cacti
magnolia	**13.** magnolia	crisantemo	**31.** chrysanthemum/	enredadera	**48.** vine
olmo	**14.** elm		mum	hierba/yerba	**49.** grass
cerezo	**15.** cherry	narciso	**32.** daffodil	hiedra/yedra	**50.** poison ivy
palma	**16.** palm	margarita	**33.** daisy	venenosa/ortiga	
abedul	**17.** birch	gardenia	**34.** gardenia		
arce	**18.** maple	lirio	**35.** lily		

[11–22]
A. What kind of tree is that?
B. I think it's a/an _____ tree.

[31–48]
A. Look at all the _____s!
B. They're beautiful!

Describe your favorite tree and your favorite flower.
What kinds of trees and flowers grow where you live?

In your country, are flowers used at weddings? at funerals?
on holidays? on visits to the hospital? Tell which flowers are
used for different occasions.

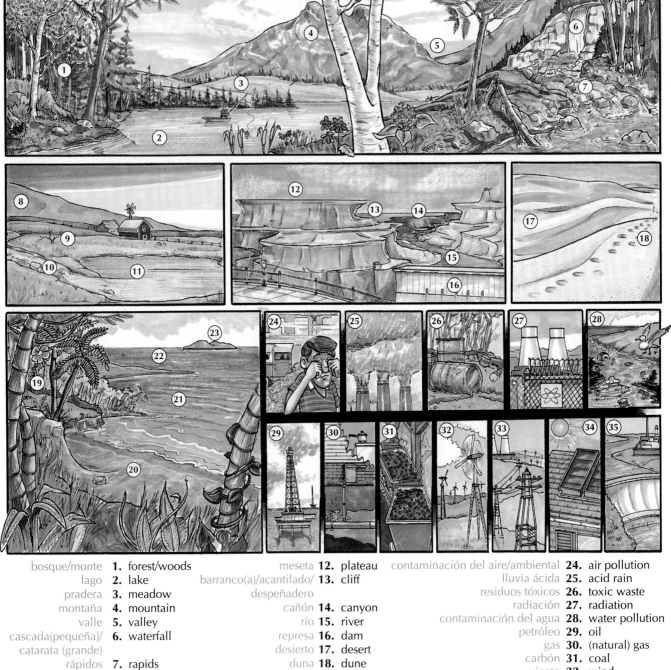

bosque/monte	**1.** forest/woods	meseta	**12.** plateau	contaminación del aire/ambiental	**24.** air pollution
lago	**2.** lake	barranco(a)/acantilado/	**13.** cliff	lluvia ácida	**25.** acid rain
pradera	**3.** meadow	despeñadero		residuos tóxicos	**26.** toxic waste
montaña	**4.** mountain	cañón	**14.** canyon	radiación	**27.** radiation
valle	**5.** valley	río	**15.** river	contaminación del agua	**28.** water pollution
cascada(pequeña)/	**6.** waterfall	represa	**16.** dam	petróleo	**29.** oil
catarata (grande)		desierto	**17.** desert	gas	**30.** (natural) gas
rápidos	**7.** rapids	duna	**18.** dune	carbón	**31.** coal
colina	**8.** hill	selva	**19.** jungle	viento	**32.** wind
campo	**9.** field	playa	**20.** seashore	energía nuclear	**33.** nuclear energy
quebrada/arroyo/	**10.** stream/brook	bahía	**21.** bay	energía solar	**34.** solar energy
arroyuelo/riachuelo		océano	**22.** ocean	hidroenergía/energía	**35.** hydroelectric
estanque/charca	**11.** pond	isla	**23.** island	hidráulica/hydroelétrica	power

[1–23]
A. { Isn't this a beautiful _____?!
     { Aren't these beautiful _____?!
B. It's/They're magnificent.

[24–28]   A.   Do you worry about the environment?
          B.   Yes. I'm very concerned about _____.

Describe some places of natural beauty in your country.

What kind of energy do you use to heat your home? to cook?
In your opinion, which kind of energy is best for producing electricity?

finca/casa	**1.** farmhouse	campo	**13.** field	pollo/gallina	**25.** chicken/hen
huerta/huerto	**2.** (vegetable) garden	segadora	**14.** combine	pollito	**26.** chick
espantapájaros	**3.** scarecrow	trilladora/cosechadora		pavo	**27.** turkey
cosecha	**4.** crop	dehesa/pasto	**15.** pasture	cabra/chivo	**28.** goat
sistema de irrigación/	**5.** irrigation system	huerto/huerta	**16.** orchard	chivo/chivito/cabrito	**29.** kid
de riego		árbol frutal/de fruta	**17.** fruit tree	carnero/oveja/borrego	**30.** sheep
granero	**6.** barn	granjero/agricultor	**18.** farmer	cordero	**31.** lamb
silo	**7.** silo	peón	**19.** hired hand	toro	**32.** bull
establo	**8.** stable	gallinero	**20.** chicken coop	vaca lechera	**33.** (dairy) cow
paja	**9.** hay	gallinero/caseta	**21.** hen house	ternero/becerro	**34.** calf–calves
trinche	**10.** pitchfork	para las gallinas		caballo	**35.** horse
corral	**11.** barnyard	cerca/valla	**22.** fence	cerdo/puerco/marrano/cochino	**36.** pig
pocilga	**12.** pig pen/pig sty	tractor	**23.** tractor	lechón/puerquito/	**37.** piglet
		gallo	**24.** rooster	cochino/cochinito	

A. Where's the _____?
B. In/On/Next to the _____.

A. The [24–37] s got loose again!
B. Oh, no! Where are they?
A. They're in the [1, 2, 12, 13, 15, 16, 20, 21] !

Tell about farms in your country.
What crops and animals are common on these farms?

ANIMALES Y MASCOTAS

zorro(a)	**1.** fox	castor	**14.** beaver	leopardo	**27.** leopard
puercoespín	**2. porcupine**	murciélago	**15.** bat	manchas	**a.** spots
púa	**a.** quill	mofeta/zorrillo	**16.** skunk	jirafa	**28.** giraffe
mapache	**3.** raccoon	marsupial/zarigüeya	**17.** possum	bisonte	**29.** bison
lobo–lobos	**4.** wolf–wolves	burro	**18.** donkey	elefante	**30.** elephant
alce	**5.** moose	búfalo	**19.** buffalo	colmillo	**a.** tusk
cuerno(a)/asta	**a.** antler	camello	**20.** camel	trompa	**b.** trunk
venado(a)/ciervo(a)	**6.** deer	joroba	**a.** hump	tigre	**31.** tiger
pezuña	**a.** hoof	llama	**21.** llama	pata/garra	**a.** paw
cervato/	**7.** fawn	caballo	**22.** horse	león	**32.** lion
cervatillo/venadito		cola	**a.** tail	melena	**a.** mane
ratón–ratones	**8.** mouse–mice	potro	**23.** foal	hipopótamo	**33.** hippopotamus
ardilla listada/rayada	**9.** chipmunk	poni	**24.** pony	hiena	**34.** hyena
rata	**10.** rat	armadillo	**25.** armadillo	rinoceronte	**35.** rhinoceros
ardilla	**11.** squirrel	canguro	**26.** kangaroo	cuerno	**a.** horn
conejo	**12.** rabbit	bolsa	**a.** pouch	zebra	**36.** zebra
topo	**13.** gopher			rayas	**a.** stripes

						Mascotas	Pets
oso negro	**37.** black bear		gibón	**44.** gibbon		**Mascotas**	**Pets**
garra	**a.** claw		mandril	**45.** baboon		gato	**51.** cat
oso parado	**38.** grizzly bear		orangután	**46.** orangutan		bigotes	**a.** whiskers
oso polar	**39.** polar bear		gorila	**47.** gorilla		gatito/cachorro	**52.** kitten
koala	**40.** koala (bear)		oso hormiguero	**48.** anteater		perro	**53.** dog
panda	**41.** panda		lombriz	**49.** worm		cachorro	**54.** puppy
mono	**42.** monkey		babosa	**50.** slug		hamster	**55.** hamster
chimpancé	**43.** chimpanzee					jerbo	**56.** gerbil
						cabayo/conejillo de indias/cui	**57.** guinea pig

[1–50] A. Look at that _____!
B. Wow! That's the biggest _____ I've ever seen!

[51–57] A. Do you have a pet?
B. Yes. I have a _____.
A. What's your _____'s name?
B. …………

What animals can be found where you live?
Is there a zoo near where you live? What animals does the zoo have?
What are some common pets in your country?

If you were an animal, which animal do you think you would be? Why?
Does your culture have any popular folk tales or children's stories about animals? Tell a story you are familiar with.

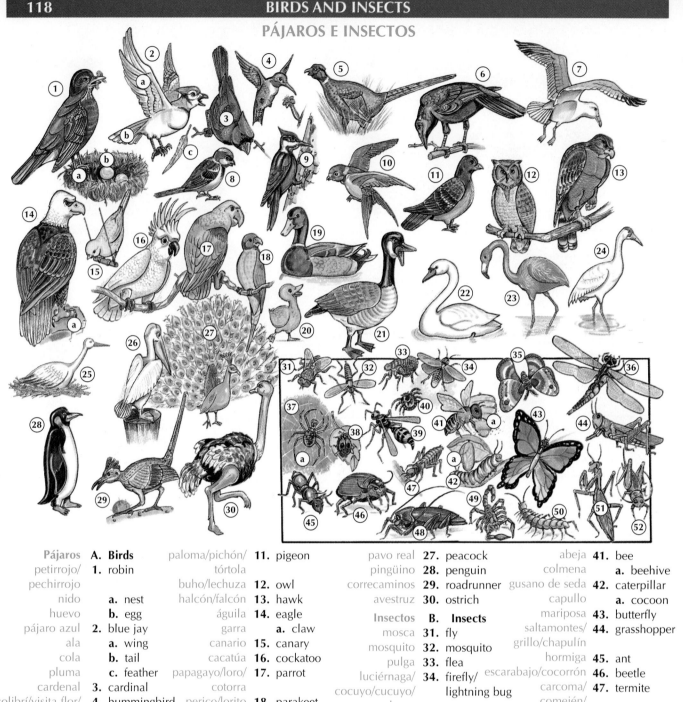

Pájaros	A.	**Birds**	paloma/pichón/	11.	pigeon
petirrojo/	1.	robin	tórtola		
pechirrojo			buho/lechuza	12.	owl
nido		**a.** nest	halcón/falcón	13.	hawk
huevo		**b.** egg	águila	14.	eagle
pájaro azul	2.	blue jay	garra		**a.** claw
ala		**a.** wing	canario	15.	canary
cola		**b.** tail	cacatúa	16.	cockatoo
pluma		**c.** feather	papagayo/loro/	17.	parrot
cardenal	3.	cardinal	cotorra		
colibrí/visita flor/	4.	hummingbird	perico/lorito	18.	parakeet
picaflor			pato	19.	duck
faisán	5.	pheasant	pico		**a.** bill
cuervo	6.	crow	patito	20.	duckling
gaviota	7.	seagull	ganso	21.	goose
gorrión/tierrerita	8.	sparrow	cisne	22.	swan
pájaro carpintero	9.	woodpecker	flamenco	23.	flamingo
pico		**a.** beak	grulla	24.	crane
golondrina	10.	swallow	cigüeña	25.	stork
			pelícano	26.	pelican

pavo real	27.	peacock
pingüino	28.	penguin
correcaminos	29.	roadrunner
avestruz	30.	ostrich
Insectos	**B.**	**Insects**
mosca	31.	fly
mosquito	32.	mosquito
pulga	33.	flea
luciérnaga/	34.	firefly/
cocuyo/cucuyo/		lightning bug
cucubano		
polilla	35.	moth
libélula/caballito	36.	dragonfly
del diablo/caballito		
de San Pedro		
araña	37.	spider
telaraña		**a.** web
mariquita/catarina/	38.	ladybug
catarinita		
avispa	39.	wasp
garrapata	40.	tick

abeja	41.	bee
colmena		**a.** beehive
gusano de seda	42.	caterpillar
capullo		**a.** cocoon
mariposa	43.	butterfly
saltamontes/	44.	grasshopper
grillo/chapulín		
hormiga	45.	ant
escarabajo/cocorrón	46.	beetle
carcoma/	47.	termite
comején/		
termita/termite/termes		
cucaracha	48.	roach/
		cockroach
escorpión/alacrán	49.	scorpion
ciempiés	50.	centipede
Mariapalito/mantis	51.	praying mantis
grillo/cigarra/	52.	cricket
chicharra		

[31–52] A. Hold still! There's a _____ on your shirt!
B. Oh! Can you get it off of me?
A. There! It's gone!

[1–52] A. Is that a/an _____?
B. No. I think it's a/an _____.

What birds and insects can be found where you live?

Does your culture have any popular folk tales or children's stories about birds or insects? Tell a story you are familiar with.

Peces	**A. Fish**	aguamala/medusa/aguaviva	**12.** jellyfish	Anfibios y reptiles	**C. Amphibians and Reptiles**
trucha	**1.** trout	nutria	**13.** otter		
aleta	**a.** fin	morsa/león de mar	**14.** walrus	tortuga	**26.** tortoise
agalla/branquia	**b.** gill	colmillo	**a.** tusk	carapacho/caparazón	**a.** shell
cola	**c.** tail	langosta	**15.** lobster	tortuga	**27.** turtle
róbalo	**2.** bass	pinza/tenaza	**a.** claw	caimán/lagarto	**28.** alligator
salmón	**3.** salmon	cangrejo	**16.** crab	cocodrilo	**29.** crocodile
tiburón	**4.** shark	pulpo	**17.** octopus	lagartija	**30.** lizard
lenguado	**5.** flounder	tentáculo	**a.** tentacle	iguana	**31.** iguana
pez espada	**6.** swordfish	camarón	**18.** shrimp	renacuajo/gusarapo	**32.** tadpole
anguila	**7.** eel	mejillón	**19.** mussel	rana	**33.** frog
caballito de mar	**8.** sea horse	almeja	**20.** clam	salamandra	**34.** salamander
Animales marinos	**B. Sea Animals**	conchuela/vieira/venera	**21.** scallop	culebra/serpiente/víbora	**35.** snake
ballena	**9.** whale	ostra	**22.** oyster		
delfín	**10.** dolphin	caracol	**23.** snail	culebra cascabel	**36.** rattlesnake
foca	**11.** seal	estrella de mar	**24.** starfish	cobra	**37.** cobra
aleta	**a.** flipper	calamar	**25.** squid	boa	**38.** boa constrictor

[1–38] A. Is that a/an _____?
B. No. I think it's a/an _____.

[26–38] A. Are there any _____s around here?
B. No. But there are lots of _____s.

What fish, sea animals, and reptiles can be found in your country?
Which ones are endangered and need to be protected? Why?

In your opinion, which ones are the most interesting?
the most beautiful? the most dangerous?

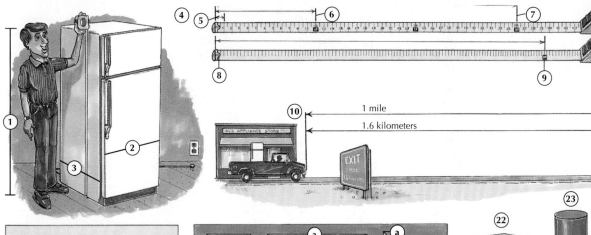

1 mile
1.6 kilometers

Medidas	A. Measurements			
alto	1. height
ancho	2. width
profundidad	3. depth
largo	4. length
pulgada	5. inch
pie/pies	6. foot–feet
yarda	7. yard
centímetro	8. centimeter
metro	9. meter
distancia	10. distance
milla	11. mile
kilómetro	12. kilometer
Líneas	**B. Lines**
línea recta	13. straight line

líneas paralelas	14. parallel lines
líneas	15. perpendicular
perpendiculares	lines
Formas geométricas	**C. Geometric Shapes**
cuadrado	16. square
lado	a. side
rectángulo	17. rectangle
largo	a. length
ancho	b. width
diagonal	c. diagonal
ángulo recto	18. right triangle
vértice	a. apex
ángulo recto	b. right angle
base	c. base
hipotenusa	d. hypotenuse

triángulo isósceles	19. isosceles triangle
ángulo agudo	a. acute angle
ángulo obtuso	b. obtuse angle
círculo	20. circle
centro	a. center
radio	b. radius
diámetro	c. diameter
circunferencia	d. circumference
elipse	21. ellipse/oval
Sólidos	**D. Solid Figures**
cubo	22. cube
cilindro	23. cylinder
esfera	24. sphere
cono	25. cone
pirámide	26. pyramid

[1–9]
A. What's the [1–4] ?
B. .... [5–9] (s).

[11–12]
A. What's the distance?
B. .... _____(s).

1 inch (1")	=	2.54 centimeters (cm)
1 foot (1')	=	0.305 meters (m)
1 yard (1 yd.)	=	0.914 meters (m)
1 mile (mi.)	=	1.6 kilometers (km)

[16–21]
A. Who can tell me what
    shape this is?
B. I can. It's a/an _____.

[22–26]
A. Who knows what figure
    this is?
B. I do. It's a/an _____.

[13–26]
A. This painting is magnificent!
B. Hmm. I don't think so. It just
    looks like a lot of _____s
    and _____s to me!

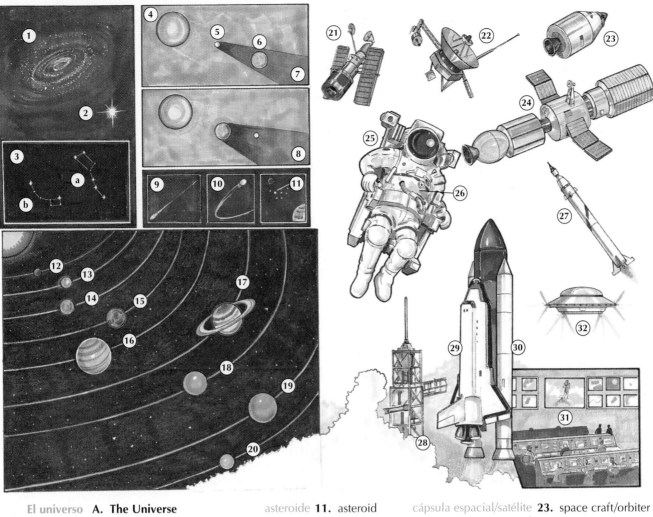

El universo	**A. The Universe**
galaxia	**1.** galaxy
estrella	**2.** star
constelación	**3.** constellation
La Osa mayor	**a.** The Big Dipper
La Osa menor	**b.** The Little Dipper

El sistema solar	**B. The Solar System**
sol	**4.** sun
luna	**5.** moon
planeta	**6.** planet
eclipse solar	**7.** solar eclipse
eclipse lunar	**8.** lunar eclipse
meteoro	**9.** meteor
cometa	**10.** comet

asteroide	**11.** asteroid
Mercurio	**12.** Mercury
Venus	**13.** Venus
tierra, La	**14.** Earth
Marte	**15.** Mars
Júpiter	**16.** Jupiter
Saturno	**17.** Saturn
Urano	**18.** Uranus
Neptuno	**19.** Neptune
Plutón	**20.** Pluto

La exploración espacial	**C. Space Exploration**
satélite	**21.** satellite
sonda espacial	**22.** (space) probe

cápsula espacial/satélite	**23.** space craft/orbiter
estación espacial	**24.** space station
astronauta	**25.** astronaut
traje espacial	**26.** space suit
cohete	**27.** rocket
plataforma de despegue/	**28.** launch pad
plataforma de lanzamiento	
transbordador/nave espacial	**29.** space shuttle
cohete retropropulsor/	**30.** booster rocket
cohete de retropropulsión	
centro de controles	**31.** mission control
platillo volador/	**32.** U.F.O./
UFO/OVNI/	Unidentified/Flying
platillo volante	Object/flying saucer

[1–20]

A. Is that (a/an/the) _____?

B. I'm not sure. I think it might be (a/an/the) _____.

[21–27, 29, 31]

A. Is the _____ ready for tomorrow's launch?

B. Yes. "All systems are go!"

Pretend you are an astronaut traveling in space.
   What do you see?
Draw and name a constellation you are familiar with.

Do you think space exploration is important? Why?
Have you ever seen a U.F.O.? Do you believe there is
   life in outer space? Why?

GLOSARIO

El número en negritas indica la página donde aparece la palabra; el número que sigue indica donde se encuentra la palabra en la ilustración y en la lista de palabras. Por ejemplo, "norte **5**-1" indica que la palabra *norte* está en la página 5 y es la primera entrada.

frustrado(a) **43**-18
fruta bomba **44**-9
fruta enlatada **46**-18
fucsia **56**-17
fuente **86**-11, **100**-11
fuente de agua **62**-9,
  100-9
fuente honda **15**-9
fumigador **27**-11
funda **17**-4
furgoneta **91**-22
furgoneta de repartos
  93-91
furioso(a) **43**-19, 20
fuselaje **97**-37
fusibles **29**-27
fútbol **105**-4
fútbol americano
  79-26, **105**-C
fútbol soccer **105**-H
futbolista **104**-15

gabán **59**-13
gabardina **59**-23
gabinete **18**-14, **22**-19,
  30, **86**-7
gafas de buceo sin
  tanque **107**-12
gafas de sol **101**-26
gafas oscuras **101**-26
gafas protectoras **90**-4
gafas protectoras de ojos
  102-26
gafas saltonas **102**-12
galaxia **121**-1
galletas **46**-20
galletas de soda **46**-21
galletas tostados cubier-
  tas con sal **48**-20
gallina **47**-38, **115**-20,
  21
gallinero **110**-16,
  115-20, 21
gallo **115**-24
galón **51**-23
gancho **89**-1
gancho de colgar **24**-29
gancho de tejer **109**-11
gancho chato para
  papeles **89**-4
gancho plástico para
  papeles **89**-2
ganchos para el cabello
  33-15
ganchos para tender
  ropa **24**-39
ganso **118**-21
garaje **25**-16, **26**-17,
  36-13, **62**-10, 20
gardenia **113**-34
garganta **69**-72
garganta inflamada **70**-6
garita de peaje **94**-3
garlopa **28**-19

garra **117**-37a, **118**-14a
garrapata **118**-4b
gas **114**-30
gasa **72**-24
gaseosa **46**-35, **54**-15
gasolinera **35**-25
gatito **117**-52
gato **117**-51
gaveta de hielo **18**-30
gavetera **17**-17, **20**-3
gavetero **17**-17, **20**-3
gaviota **118**-7
gelatina **55**-28
gemelos **60**-12
geografía **78**-8
geometría **78**-3
gerente **86**-31
gibón **117**-44
gimnasia **103**-T
gimnasio **35**-29, **77**-11
ginecólogo **72**-9
giradiscos **63**-7
girasol **113**-40
giro postal **67**-11, **75**-15
gis **10**-19
globo del mundo **10**-27
globo terráqueo **10**-27
golf **102**-J
golondrina **118**-10
golpearse (me golpeé)
  71-44, 47
goma **89**-7, 24, **101**-23
goma de mascar **49**-87
goma de masticar
  49-87
goma de pegar **29**-30
goma en barra **89**-23
goma de borrar **10**-7
goma para armar
  modelos **109**-23
goma sintética **89**-25
gordo(a) **40**-9
gorila **117**-47
gorra **59**-28
gorra de baño **23**-8,
  101-13, **107**-18
gorra de béisbol **59**-29
gorrión **118**-8
gorro **59**-32
gorro de baño **23**-8
gorro de esquiar **59**-32
gospel **111**-7
gota para los ojos **74**-9
gotera **25**-19
grabadora **87**-10
grabadora de cintas
  63-14
grabadora de cintas
  magnetofónicas **63**-14
gradas **77**-15
grande **40**-5, **61**-5
gradería **77**-15
granero **115**-6
granizando **98**-11

granja **13**-8
granjero **81**-23, **115**-18
grapa **89**-8
grifo **18**-4
grillo **118**-44, 52
gripe **70**-8
gris **56**-10
grúa **91**-17, **93**-92
grueso(a) **40**-23, **61**-11
grulla **118**-24
guagua **38**-15, **95**-18
guante **102**-102, **105**-6,
  9
guante de catcher **105**-7
guante de hockey
  105-19
guante de receptor
  105-7
guantera **93**-67
guantes **59**-25, **72**-21
guantes de boxeo
  103-50
guantes de jardín **29**-13
guantes enteros **59**-26
guapo(a) **41**-53
guarda **67**-16, **83**-19,
  96-6
guardar cama **73**-9
guarde(n) el libro **11**-10
guardería infantil **34**-9
guardia de seguridad
  67-16, **83**-19, **96**-6
guía **62**-1, **93**-5, **110**-17
guía de terreno **109**-26
guillotina **87**-18
güila **101**-21
guineo **44**-4
guisante **45**-13
guise(a) **53**-8
guitarra (acústica) **112**-5
guitarra eléctrica **112**-7
gusano de seda **118**-42
gusarapo **119**-32

haba **45**-15
habichuelas coloradas
  45-17
habichuelas tiernas
  45-14
hacendado **81**-23
hacer alpinismo **99**-C
hacer bobsleigh **106**-F
hacer buceo submarino
  107-H
hacer colchas **109**-G
hacer ejercicios **9**-20,
  73-11
hacer el almuerzo **8**-17
hacer el desayuno **8**-16
hacer escalada **99**-D
hacer esquí alpino
  106-A
hacer esquí de fondo
  106-B

hacer esquí nórdico
  106-B
hacer footing **102**-A
hacer gárgaras **73**-12
hacer la cama **8**-11
hacer la cena **8**-18
hacer montañismo **99**-C
hacer plancha de vela
  107-J
hacer tejido de punto
  109-B
hacer tejido en punto de
  cruz **109**-E
hacer travesía en moto
  de nieve **106**-G
hacer(hago) cosas **84**-4
hacha **28**-7, **99**-5
hacienda **13**-8
haga(n) clavados
  108-27
haga(n) su tarea **11**-16
halcón **118**-13
hale(n) **108**-24
hamburguesa **54**-8
hamburguesa con queso
  54-9
hamster **117**-55
handbol **102**-M
harina **48**-43
harmónica **112**-33
harto(a) **43**-13
hastiado(a) **42**-13
haz flexiones **108**-12
hebillas de cabello
  23-17
hechuras de pino
  108-36
heladería **36**-2
helado **47**-75, **55**-27,
  98-25
helando **98**-12
helecho **113**-45
hélice **97**-44
helicóptero **97**-45
hemorragia nasal **70**-17
hermana **2**-7
hermano **2**-8
hervidor **19**-21
hidroenergía **114**-35
hiedra venenosa
  113-50
hielera **101**-31
hiena **116**-34
hierba **113**-49
hierva(e) **53**-18
hígado **69**-68
higiene **78**-16
higienista **72**-7
higo **44**-11
hija **2**-5
hijo **2**-6
hilar **109**-C
hilo **109**-4, 9
hilo de dientes **23**-23

hilo dental **23**-23
hinchado (a) **71**-30
hipo **70**-20
hipopótamo **116**-33
hipoteca **27**-21
hipotenusa **120**-18d
hisopos **21**-8
historia **78**-7
hockey sobre hielo
  105-E
hogar **14**-24
hogaza de pan **51**-13
hoja **112**-2
hoja clínica **73**-26
hoja de asistencia
  88-24
hojas **112**-2
hojuelas **48**-21
hombreras **24**-49
hombro **68**-28, **94**-17
hongo **45**-23
horario **88**-14, **95**-5
hormiga **118**-45
hormigonera **91**-19
hornear (horneo) **84**-3
hornée(a) **53**-17
hornilla **18**-20, **99**-7
hornillo **18**-19, 20
hornito **19**-22
horno **18**-21
horno microondas
  18-15
horno pastelero **19**-22
horquillas de tender
  ropa **24**-39
horquillas para el ca
  bello **23**-16
hospital **35**-30
hot dog **54**-10
hotel **36**-1
huerta **115**-2, 16
huerto **115**-3, 16
huesos **69**-74
huevo **118**-16
huevos **46**-14
hula hoop **65**-8
húmedo **98**-7
huracán **98**-16

iguana **119**-31
imperdibles **21**-9
impermeable **59**-21, 23
impresora **64**-6
impresora con mecanis-
  mo de máquina de
  escribir **87**-3
impresora de alta cali-
  dad **87**-4
impresora laser **87**-5
impresos **75**-8
inchado **71**-49
indicador de gasolina
  93-49
indicador de rutas **94**-5

GLOSSARY

The bold number indicates the page(s) on which the word appears; the number that follows indicates the word's location in the illustration and in the word list on the page. For example, "north **5**-1" indicates that the word *north* is on page 5 and is item number 1.

THEMATIC INDEX / ÍNDICE TEMÁTICO